MEDIEVAL AND RENAISSANCE DAGGER COMBAT

MEDIEVAL AND RENAISSANCE DAGGER COMBAT

JASON VAIL

PALADIN PRESS • BOULDER, COLORADO

Medieval and Renaissance Dagger Combat
by Jason Vail

Copyright © 2006 by Jason Vail

ISBN 13: 978-1-58160-517-4
Printed in the United States of America
Published by Paladin Press, a division of

Paladin Enterprises, Inc.
Gunbarrel Tech Center
7077 Winchester Circle
Boulder, Colorado 80301 USA
+1.303.443.7250
Direct inquiries and/or orders to the above address.

Cover illustration: Detail from the Maceijowski Bible (Pierpont Morgan Library MS. M. 638 fol. 36v, Zone 1: *Abner and Joab: at Pool of Gibeon*), with permission of the Pierpont Morgan Library, 225 Madison Ave., New York, NY 10016. (www.themorgan.org.)

TABLE OF CONTENTS

ACKNOWLEDGMENTS

The author wishes to thank Jack and Linda Morris of American Karate Studios, Tallahassee, Florida, for donating the use of their facility to complete the principle photography for this book. The author wishes to thank Erwin Bodo, a real Renaissance man and great intellect, who took the pictures. The author also wishes to thank his partner in the photos, Steve Shaffer, a third-degree black belt in American Kenpo, U.S. Army veteran, and gifted martial artist who has been on his own journey through the martial arts since the 1970s. Although Steve has chosen to follow a different path than me, his comments and insights have been helpful in interpreting the ancient texts for the modern martial artist.

Thanks to Michael Shire of the Knights of the Wild Rose, Calgary, Canada, for permission to use his scans of the illustrations from Fiore Dei Liberi's *Flos Duellatorum*, the Pisani-Dossi version. I'd like to thank my son, Sam Vail, for the sketches of historical daggers.

Mere words cannot convey the gratitude the author feels toward the members of the Association for Renaissance Martial Arts (ARMA). They, and in particular John Clements, have opened up a whole new, productive field of study in the martial arts that has expanded my horizons beyond the often blinkered confines of style or system in which we, as martial artists, often find ourselves trapped.

Also, there are my training partners, on whom I experimented with my interpretations of the texts. They are many and so will remain anonymous. But I thank them, for without their sometimes-unknowing help, this book would not have been possible.

FOREWORD

Most people do not seriously consider how they could secure themselves against all manner of abuse or assault, as might be leveled against them by evil hearted villains, eager for violence.
—Nicolaes Petter, 1674

Few weapons are as common and ever-present in history as knives. For soldier and civilian alike during the medieval and Renaissance eras a small-handled, short-bladed weapon for cutting, thrusting, or cutting and thrusting was an all but compulsory companion. Of all the weapons from the medieval and Renaissance eras, the fighting dagger is today the most relevant to modern self-defense and battlefield application. It is by far the most likely of archaic weapons still to be encountered.

In earlier, more brutal times, a dagger was to a sword, in a sense, what today a handgun is to an assault rifle. Both will kill a person just as decisively, but each has its role and its place. Just as not everyone who carries a handgun today is a crack shot or a highly trained marksman, so too not everyone who once wore a dagger was expert in its use. But expert teachers in arms existed

throughout the Middle Ages and the Renaissance, and they produced numerous detailed treatises on every kind of weapon, especially the dagger. While new combat knife designs come out every year, it seems there is little new in terms of fighting with them that was not already addressed in their little-known instructional manuals.

Despite the prevalence of knives and daggers in the modern world and their continued popularity among collectors, martial artists, soldiers, paramilitaries, knife fighters, and bladesmiths, little to nothing has been known of the vast literature produced on the subject by masters of defence in Western Europe from the 14th to 17th centuries. Although there has been a substantial interest in knife fighting for decades, surprisingly little of this heritage has been seriously studied in modern times because this unique material has for so long remained obscure. Regardless, the volume of dagger-fighting material within the extensive source literature of historical European martial arts represents an essential part of the Western tradition of systematically recording study guides in images and text on virtually all arts and sciences. These teachings are substantial and feature techniques developed and proven over generations.

For centuries the dagger was a common instrument for most any man (and many women) to carry. For close combat, whether in war or duel, streetfight, tavern brawl, or ambuscade, the dagger was an obligatory item of equipment for noble and commoner alike. As one 14th-century poem reads, "There is no man worth a leke, Be he sturdy or be he meke, But he bear a basilard." It was a tool, it was a utensil, and it was a fearsome weapon. For battlefield combat or civilian self-defense the variety of specialized knives and daggers designs produced were formidable and lethal. They were fashioned with all manners of blades and styles of hilt ranging from the plain and unremarkable to the richly ornate. Whether a pick-like anti-armor type, a long narrow poniard for parrying, a short, slender, and well-concealed stiletto or bodkin, a heavy fighting dirk, or a wide, single-edged slashing and stabbing knife, they came in all shapes and sizes.

Occurrences of dagger fighting fill historical accounts of medieval and Renaissance combat, testifying to the weapon's popularity and utility. Remarking on the Parisian "town and gown" brawls in the early 1200s, Philip Augustus recorded he "was impressed by the readiness of the tonsured clerics of the University for street brawling," declaring, "They are hardier than knights for even armored knights hesitate to engage in battle. These clerks, having neither hauberk nor helmet, throw themselves into the fight armed only with daggers."[1]

An armored knight was a difficult opponent to overcome in battle but, having closed to grappling range, a fighter could find that a dagger designed to pierce his more vulnerable spots could make all the difference. A medieval warrior in full plate armor was effectively immune to sharp blows of wide-bladed cutting swords, but in close combat he was vulnerable to special-ized crushing weapons and to thrusts from tapering swords and to sharp, stabbing daggers jammed into the joints and gaps of his armor. If he fell to the ground he could be killed just like any other fallen opponent, and a favored technique was piercing him in a vulnerable spot with a dagger thrust into his helmet openings, underarm, or groin (a knife used in this manner was sometimes called a *miséricorde*, perhaps because it put mortally wounded men out of their misery or made them beg for mercy). In fighting against the English as described in the 15th-century chronicle of the deeds of the Spanish knight, Don Pero Niño, we are told for example how armored fighters "come to grips one with the other or take to their daggers; some fall to the ground, others rise again, and blood flowing abundantly in many places."[2] Even on horseback, when two armored riders were too close for lances, swords, or axes and maces, the daggers came out immediately as the logical choice. Several accounts of daggers being effectively thrown during duels or streetfights are also known. A plate from the 1467 edition of Hans Talhoffer's fight book even shows a figure having thrown first his hat at an attacker's face to momentarily obscure his eyesight, then lobbing his dagger into the man's chest before the man could run him through with a spear.

During the early 1500s, the famed artist Benvenuto Cellini described assaulting his rival, Pompeo, in Rome: "I drew a little dagger and broke through the line of his defenders so quickly and coolly that none was able to prevent me. I aimed to strike Pompeo in the face, but he turned his head in fright and I stabbed him just beneath the ear. I only gave two blows, for he fell stone dead at the second. I had not meant to kill him, but as the saying goes, knocks are not dealt by measure."[3] Even in the notorious 1547 judicial duel between the nobles Jarnac and Châtaigneraie, Jarnac had been so concerned at Châtaigneraie's well-known skill as a wrestler (not to mention as a fencer) that to avoid any chance of a close struggle, he insisted both parties each wear two daggers. A larger dagger was fastened by cords to the right thigh with the point going in the high boot. The smaller one was placed on the left leg inserted between the boot and the stocking. This would give him at least a better chance should he be disarmed, thrown down, or jumped. Châtaigneraie had in fact won several previous duels precisely by rushing his opponents and wrestling them to the ground where he killed them with his dagger. Jarnac's precautions helped keep his opponent away, and he defeated him with sword cuts to the leg.

The historical accounts are filled with references to daggers and their use. In the late 16th century, the Comte Mortinengo even fought a dagger duel against another noble alone on a narrow bridge in the city of Pau in Piedmont. Both combatants wielded two daggers, one in each hand, while also wearing a stiff armored bracer on one arm. From Olaus Magnus' early 16th century *Description of the Northern Peoples*, we read of how, "In close quarters ... they use many different kinds of dagger and poniard, the narrow type, that is, and the broad, some two-edged, some curved or hooked."[4] In 1555 Claude Haton wrote, "There was no mother's son at this time who did not carry a sword or a dagger," while in 1587 William Harrison stated, "Not many traveleth by the way without his sword or some such weapon with us except the minister, who commonly weareth none at all unless it be a dagger or hanger at his side." An English Sumptuary Statute of 1562 even tried to outlaw weapons of excessive length, forbidding among other items, "any dagger above the length of twelve inches in blade."[5] But in his 1617, *School of the Noble and Worthy Science of Defence*, the English Master Joseph Swetnam recommended a dagger of 22 inches for use alone or with a rapier or backsword. In 16th-

century France, distinctions between nobles and commoners were not that clearly recognized when it came to dueling with the dagger such that, while a French gentleman would not even think to fight a sword duel with his social inferior, he would freely fight him with a dagger.

The lore of the dagger is long and rich. While the sword was traditionally praised and prized as heroic and noble, the dagger more often has come to be viewed as something of a lowly cousin. It was a necessary retainer and loyal follower but never quite the courageous leader.

Perhaps it was the knowledge that even an armored knight could be dispatched with one that awarded the weapon such stigma. Perhaps it was the ability of such a small weapon to be readily concealed yet drawn suddenly and used quickly that it came to be viewed with such dread. Or perchance it was simply a result of understanding the difficulty any fighting man would have in defending himself when confronted by surprise with such a fast and lethal tool. The word dagger itself, from the Middle English *daggere* and root *dague*, meaning to stab or pierce, even now connotes deception and underhandedness. But its origin may be related to the French word *dague*, Italian *daga*, or the German *dolch* or *degen* (a kind of sword). In 1348 an Englishman wrote of seeing women spectators at knightly tournaments wearing small knives called *daggerios*.

Whatever the reasons, daggers and other fighting knives eventually became associated with the lowest elements of society—who still had need to carry them for their labor or concealed on their persons for more illicit reasons. The very phrase "cloak-and-dagger," today connoting intrigue, subterfuge, or espionage, comes from this time, referring to the stealthy, skulking culprit hiding in shadows and back alleys. Still today "to look daggers" or "speak daggers" at someone is an old phrase meaning to speak or glare so as to wound the sensibilities, such as

Shakespeare's "I will speak daggers to her, but will use none" (*Hamlet*, act III, scene II).

By the 16th century a versatile combination style of sword and dagger fencing was prevalent both for war and urban street fighting. In time this became the rapier and dagger method so popular for single combat and dueling across Western Europe. The dagger continued to find application in conjunction with both styles throughout the 17th and into the 18th centuries. However, as firearms became more prevalent and travel somewhat safer, the function of a dagger for common protection and military utility declined ever more (even as the first bayonets were themselves forms of detachable dagger). Fencing itself soon came to no longer reflect a variety of weapons and swords used with daggers and shields or armors, or skill in close grappling or facing multiple opponents, but narrowed into ritualized single-combat duels with matching single swords. The later advent of the lighter, quicker, smallsword as a gentleman's sidearm for duelling did not on its own cause the dagger to somehow vanish as an "unnecessary" defensive weapon. Rather, it was the dagger's social status and close-in lethality that discouraged its use among Baroque duelists who had other cultural motivations influencing their fencing choices for single-combat besides pure martial effectiveness. Daggers, being shorter and lighter than swords, are extremely dangerous and difficult to combat when in close. Doing away with them in 18th-century civilian swordplay helped reduce the lethality of formal duels and made the ritual safer for gentlemen fencers to better avoid the potentially more lethal outcomes that such weapons tended to promote. As handguns had already rendered daggers largely redundant for concealed protection, its exclusion from the poised and mannered fencing of the smallsword faded its legacy even further.

But among medieval and Renaissance fighting men, dagger-fighting skills, being so common and so deadly, in many ways served as a foundational lesson for self-defense. Its relationship to both grappling and the wielding of larger blades and staff weapons was certainly understood. In many 14th- and 15th-century judicial combats, armored knights entering the closed pen were frequently armed only with long tapering swords and rondel daggers, precisely because both weapons were deemed so decisive and versatile in such combats. Much of the material on dagger-fighting techniques within the earliest historical source literature reflects this very activity. The remainder of the works concern unarmored civilian self-defense with or against the dagger.

The method of dagger fighting revealed in these works is vicious, practical, and lucid. The reader may find many similarities to modern forms of knife fighting and to the wielding of short blades in some traditional Asian martial arts. But beside such commonalities there are many differences and distinctions reflecting the nature of the weapon, the conditions it was employed under, the temperament of the men employing it, and the theories underlying Western fencing arts.

Medieval and Renaissance daggers were also employed somewhat differently from modern fighting knives, primarily because of their design. They typically had to be large and sturdy enough to defensively encounter swords and other weapons. They also tended to be longer and configured more for thrusting as a necessity for fighting opponents wearing armor or heavily padded cloth garments. In such an environment it was generally more effective to deliver decisive puncture wounds than attempt indeterminate slashes. After all, whether made by a sword point, a spear thrust, or a dagger stab, four or five inches of steel will kill just as well.

At one time, no medieval man-at-arms or Renaissance fencing master would have been without skill at dagger fighting. It was an integrated part of the *noble science*. But, although related by core principles, the techniques and physical mechanics of dagger combat are also not entirely the same as "fencing" with swords (especially in contrast to modern conceptions of the craft). It goes without saying that there is a world of differences between the study of a diverse martial art of armed and unarmed fighting skills that included daggers, and the practice of fencing for ritual combat sport or dueling game. We might also consider that, unlike fencing with swords or other hand weapons, personal combat with daggers has an immediacy and distinct lack of pretense. It is much closer, there is little opportunity for parrying or complicated motions, there is little time to react, and little opportunity to do much more than strike lethally (though the weapon can certainly be applied in capturing rather than harming adversaries). The material presented here thus reflects the violent reality of personal self-defense in a dangerous world.

With the renewed interest in Western fighting arts now under way and serious exploration of the systematic methods of medieval and Renaissance masters of defence becoming more popular, it is by far time that the dagger again assumes its rightful role as a respected and fundamental aspect of fencing study. I am proud to be able to present here a practical guide on this weapon by an adept scholar and accomplished student of the martial arts. An overview of fighting with the dagger as practiced in the Middle Ages and Renaissance, this reconstructive interpretation is the first-ever modern work to address the wealth of sophisticated historical material on this resourceful weapon. Following the pragmatic and holistic study approach of ARMA, the Association for Renaissance Martial Arts, this work will be a valuable introduction and guide for anyone interested in the history of the dagger and the application of its authentic teachings for both historical fencing study and real-life self-defense. As a valuable contribution

toward raising the credibility and legitimacy of historical fencing studies and reestablishing the lost teachings of our Western martial heritage, I am confident in stating this work will go a long way toward that goal. It reveals a rich aspect of our Western martial heritage that is only now being accurately resurrected and credibly revived. Medieval dagger fighting is not to be understated. There is a reason why, after all, the 14th-century master of arms, Hans Talhoffer, opened his treatise's section on the weapon with the words, "Now we take up the dagger. God preserve us all!"

"Guard your self well, for every little disorder giveth advantage to your adversary"
—Master Vincentio Saviolo, 1594

John Clements
Director
ARMA, the Association
for Renaissance Martial Arts
October 2005

ENDNOTES

1. E.R. Chamberlin. *Life in Medieval France.* B.T. Batsford Ltd, 1967, pp. 115–116.
2. Gutierre Diaz De Gamez. *The Unconquered Knight: A Chronicle of the Deeds of Don Pero Niño, Count of Buelna.* Joan Evans, trans. London: George Routledge & Sons, 1928, p. 176.
3. Benvenuto Cellini. *The Autobiography of Benvenuto Cellini.* Alfred Tamarin, ed. Abridged and adapted from the translation by John Addington Symonds. London: Collier-Macmillan, Ltd., 1969, p. 43.
4. Olaus Magnus. *Historia de Gentibus Septentrionalibus* (Description of the Northern Peoples). Volume II. No. 187. Peter Fisher and Humphrey Higgins, trans. London: Hakluyt Society, 1998, p. 373.

5. Edmund Lodge. *Illustrations of British History: Biography and Manners in the Reign of Henry VIII, Edward VI, Mary, Elizabeth and James I.* G. Nicol, London, 1791, Vol. II, p. 228.

PREFACE

While there are several modern books on the form of the medieval and Renaissance dagger as well as historical swordsmanship, there are none describing how daggers were used in combat. This book is intended to remedy that deficiency. Drawing from sources written during the period 1409–1600, this book illustrates the deadly and effective techniques of European dagger fighting for the general and specialist reader.

Study of the use of the medieval dagger is not some arid academic exercise. The field has modern, real-world benefits. First, the techniques set down by the old masters were simple. Simplicity of technique is critical because complex techniques become extremely difficult, if not impossible, to perform under the stress of combat.

Second, and more important, we can be confident these techniques are effective. The manuals that form the basis for the book were written by men with real fighting experience, not self-promoted "grand masters" or denizens of the training hall. They knew what worked and sought to pass on their knowledge in writing and pictures. The result is a record of the "true stuff" that remained remarkably unchanged through 200 years of European martial literature and was consistent from Germany to Italy.

Third, the techniques used by medieval fighters are valid today; the dynamics of the fight involving small edged weapons have not changed. Although the medieval dagger was a much larger weapon than the tactical folder, many of the same basic principles apply to its use—and to defense against an attack. This is particularly true of unarmed defense. Anyone who studies Fiore dei Liberi's unarmed defenses against the dagger, set down in 1409, prepares himself to frustrate an attack by an assailant wielding a modern tactical folder.

Thus, the study of medieval dagger fighting is satisfying as the pursuit of an independent martial art by itself, and as practical preparation for modern, real-world self-defense.

CHAPTER 1

THE UBIQUITOUS DAGGER

Daggers, or more accurately knives, have been part of man's tool kit for millennia. Knives, in fact, are probably among man's first tools. The stone hand axes of the Acheulean industry date to 1.5 million years ago and probably were knives rather than axes. And even earlier, hominids used stone flakes to butcher carcasses.

Exactly when daggers—that is, hafted knives—were invented is impossible to say. But they existed in the age of stone technology and are probably very ancient, perhaps even as old as our own species, which emerged in Africa sometime before 195,000 years ago. We can surmise this from a spectacular recent find in the Italian Alps.

FROZEN IN TIME

In 1991 hikers near a mountaintop in the Ötzal Alps, not far from the border between Austria and Italy, stumbled across the mummy of a man who had died 5,300 years ago, his body and possessions frozen in the ice. That man, who has been nicknamed Ötzi, carried a small stone dagger or knife. The blade was a triangular piece of chipped flint 6.4 centimeters long including the tang. It had lost its tip and may have been 8–9 millimeters longer. It was set in an ash handle and had an overall length of 12.8 centimeters, or about 4.9 inches. The blade was so small it might have been mistaken for an arrow or javelin head if it hadn't been found with its handle.

This is a modern replica of a stone dagger similar to the one carried by Ötzi.

Indeed, many stone blades found in Europe and the Americas that are classed as arrow or spear heads may well have been knives. Ötzi wore the blade in a scabbard of intricately woven grass at his right hip.[1]

Such a small knife was probably a utility blade, but there is evidence Ötzi used it for combat. An analysis of blood on the blade found it was human and came from someone else. In addition, Ötzi had cuts on his hands—one between the thumb and index finger—consistent with defensive wounds one might receive during a knife attack. He received these wounds within 48 hours of his death; thus, some writers now theorize that he was engaged in a desperate fight shortly before he died, that it involved knives, and that Ötzi probably used his own blade to stab or cut at least one other person. Since he survived without serious wounds, whatever he did to defend himself was successful. Knife fighting, thus, almost certainly is as old as knives themselves.

A HISTORY OF VIOLENCE

Indeed, historical literature has numerous accounts of knife fights and knife attacks, and frequent historical references demonstrate how ubiquitous the knife or dagger was. It was an instrument of political assassination in classical Greece, and one of history's most significant murders, the killing of Julius Caesar in 44 BC, was carried out with daggers. Although contemporary art does not show Greek hoplites wearing daggers, such weapons must have been common appliances and were sometimes relied on in war when swords were not considered useful. For instance, during the march of the Ten Thousand out of Mesopotamia in 401 BC, the hoplite infantry reconnoitered an Anatolian ford by stripping naked and wading across the river armed only with their daggers.[2] During the Viking era, the Norse, or at least Icelanders,

often carried small utility knives in scabbards hung from cords around their necks, much like North American Indians. But long knives were common. Examples have been found in Viking burials.[3] Men used these knives, whether long or short, to attack others, and when attacked, men knew how to turn the assault to their advantage:

> Thorir had a bear-hunting knife in his hand and rushed at Ospak, lunging at him, but Ospak averted the blow. Since Thorir had thrown himself into a lunge which did not find its mark, he fell forward onto his knees with his head bent over. Ospak then struck down on Thorir's back with his axe and there was a loud crack.[4]

FAMOUS DUELS

In the medieval period, daggers often decided the outcome of knightly duels. The historical accounts of these duels are unlike anything depicted by Hollywood, which gets nothing right about historical combat. Two stories are illustrative. The first took place in 1357 at Dinan, France, during the Hundred Years' War. Bertrand de Guesclin, the future marshal of France, challenged Thomas of Canterbury after Thomas captured Guesclin's younger brother for violating a truce by riding outside the city's walls. Thomas wanted a ransom—fairly typical of the times. Guesclin, however, was so enraged that he demanded and was granted single combat. The duel took place in the city in an open area about 120 yards long. It began with lances, which soon were shattered, and continued with swords. Sword blows did not have much effect on these armored men, as was often the case. As they came close together, Guesclin grasped Thomas about the waist and attempted to throw him from the saddle.[5] During this mounted struggle, Thomas lost his grip on his sword, which fell to the ground. Guesclin released his hold, spurred his horse away, then slipped from his saddle and threw Thomas' sword out of the lists. Guesclin then began removing his leg armor, preparing to continue the fight on foot. Without his sword, Thomas apparently was unwilling to continue the duel, so he dismounted and spurred his horse in an attempt to ride Guesclin down. Guesclin traversed and stabbed Thomas' horse in the side with his dagger. According to one account Thomas' horse threw him; according to another, it collapsed and trapped him beneath its body. Guesclin sat on Thomas and beat on his helmet with a dagger. Managing to open the visor, Guesclin then pounded Thomas' face with the pommel of his dagger until Thomas submitted.[6]

A dagger thrust decided the last formal judicial duel fought in France in 1386. Jean de Carrouges accused Jacques le Gris of raping his wife, Marguerite. He demanded and ultimately received permission for trial by combat. The fight began with a joust, but without any fence separating the combatants. They made two passes without breaking a lance, but on the third pass, both lances shattered. The fight continued on horseback with axes. During the wheeling melee, le Gris struck a great, two-handed blow at Carrouges. Carrouges raised his shield in time to protect himself, but the axe head deflected from the shield and struck Carrouges' horse in the neck, killing it. Carrouges leaped clear as the horse collapsed. Le Gris charged, trying to impale Carrouges on the top spike of his axe. Carrouges leaped out of the way and thrust his own axe spike into le Gris' horse just behind the girth. Carrouges' axe head sank deeply and stuck fast in the wound, and the horse's momentum tore it from his grasp. Le Gris' horse then crumpled, and the fight continued on foot with swords, "thrusting and striking and slashing." At last, the two men nearly spent, le Gris stabbed Carrouges in the thigh. Le Gris drew his sword from the wound and stepped back as if expecting

Carrouges to fall. But Carrouges grasped le Gris by the top of his helmet and, pulling sharply forward, threw le Gris to the ground. Carrouges stood over le Gris and tried to stab through the fallen man's armor with his sword but was unable to do so.[7] Finally, when le Gris tried to strike from his fallen position, Carrouges knocked the sword from his hands and fell upon him. Kneeling on le Gris' chest, Carrouges continued to thrust with the point of his sword, but with no more success than he had had before. Reversing the blade and pounding le Gris about the head with the pommel of his sword, Carrouges succeeded in breaking the latch securing le Gris' helmet visor. Carrouges flipped up the visor and cast his sword aside because he could not hold le Gris' helmet and wield the sword at the same time. Carrouges drew his dagger. He demanded le Gris confess the rape. Le Gris cried that he was innocent. "Then be you damned!" shouted Carrouges, who then drove the point of his dagger under le Gris' jaw and into his brain.[8]

A COMMON OCCURRENCE

Dagger and knife use, of course, wasn't restricted to the knightly class. Since virtually every man of the age carried a knife or dagger, dagger fights—or more accurately dagger homicides—were common. Surviving London coroners' rolls for 1300–1378 record at least 87 homicides committed with daggers or knives. Most were sudden, one-sided attacks, but a few involved fights between armed men. Here is one such dagger-to-dagger fight, which occurred on a Sunday in mid-Lent in 1325:

The jurors say that on the preceding Sunday at the hour of Compline [about 6 p.m.] a certain William de "Wydyngtone" de Westwall and Robert, son of Walter de Glouc[estre], Knt. and the above [victim] John de

Hamertone were quarrelling together in Chepe at the Broken Shield and fought with knives and other weapons so that the said William struck the said John in the belly, through the middle of the body, with his knife called "Irisshknyf," mortally wounding him, and the said Robert struck the said John on the head and left arm with a weapon called a "misericode" inflicting two mortal wounds; that the said John so wounded fled to the church aforesaid, and sounding the bells, died.[9]

Here is another account from September 1325 about the death of a man named Nicholas Crabbe at a Thames-side wharf:

The jurors say that on the preceding Sunday, after the hour of Vespers, the said Nicholas and a certain John "Paling" of Flanders were quarrelling on the aforesaid wharf, when the said Nicholas drew his knife called "anelaz" and therewith wounded the said John four times on the throat and neck and pursued him with intent to kill him as far as the water of the Thames; that at length the said John drew his knife called "trenchour," and therewith struck the said Nicholas under the left breast to the heart so that he immediately died.[10]

John sought sanctuary in a nearby church and evidently survived his wounds.

It is hard to imagine John Paling surviving this sudden, determined attack without some knowledge of how to defend himself against it, although certainly untrained, inexperienced people have successfully defended themselves throughout history against knife and dagger attacks.

THE DEATH OF CHRISTOPHER MARLOWE

History turned on the point of a dagger on the evening of May 30, 1593, in Deptford, a village on the south bank of the Thames three miles east of London.

Christopher Marlowe, the celebrated Elizabethan poet and playwright, was drunk and angry. He lay fuming on the bed in an upstairs room of the house of the widow Elizabeth Bull. Like many widows, she rented rooms and provided meals to strangers for a little extra income. Marlowe, who had come down from London for a meeting (whose purpose has been the source of controversy since that fatal evening), had spent the day drinking and talking in the garden with three mysterious men—Robert Poley, a well-paid and trusted spy who lurked on the margins of English society; and Nicholas Skeres and Ingram Frizer, grifters and con-artists who had done so well for themselves that they got away with calling themselves gentlemen. The four men had supper in the upstairs room about 6 p.m.

After supper, according to the official account, Marlowe and Frizer argued over the contents of the bill. They exchanged harsh words—not hard to believe about Marlowe, who had a temper and a sharp and famous wit. They did not resolve the dispute.

Marlowe retired to the bed, nursing his anger, while the other three sat on a bench nearby, all three in a row, side by side with their backs to Marlowe, and played backgammon.

Marlowe watched and simmered. Finally his fury got the best of him. The coroner's report blandly records what happened next:

Christopher Morely then lying upon a bed in the room where they supped, & moved with anger against the said Ingram ffrysar upon the words aforesaid spoken between them, and the said Ingram then & there sitting in

4

the room aforesaid with his back toward the bed where the said Christopher Morely was then lying, sitting near the bed, that is, nere the bed, & and with the front part of his body toward the table & and the aforesaid Nicholas Skeres & Robert Poley Ingram ffrysar in no wise could take flight: it so befell that the said Christopher Morely on a sudden & of his malice towards the said Ingram aforethought, then & there maliciously drew the dagger of the said Ingram which was at his back, and with the same dagger the said Christopher Morely then & there maliciously gave the aforesaid Ingram two wounds on his head of the length of two inches & and of the depth of a quarter of an inch; whereupon the said Ingram, in fear of being slain, & sitting in the manner aforesaid between said Nicholas Skeres & Robert Poley so that he could not in any wise get away, in his own defence & and for the saving of his life, then & there struggled with the said Christopher Morely to get back from his dagger aforesaid; in which affray the same Ingram could not get away from the said Christopher Morely; and so it befell that in that affray that the said Ingram, in defence of his life, with the dagger aforesaid to the value of 12d. Gave the said Christopher then and there a mortal would over his right eye to the depth of two inches & of the width of one inch; of which mortal wound the aforesaid Christopher Morely then & there instantly died . . . [11]

Stripped to its essentials, the story is this: Marlowe rose from the bed, drew Frizer's own dagger, which he carried at the small of his back, and attacked Frizer from behind. It is unclear whether Marlowe tried to stab or pommel Frizer. Frizer rose to meet the attack, having nowhere to run or fight effectively, hemmed in by the bench, the table, and his two companions. Frizer and Marlowe struggled over possession of the dagger. Frizer wrestled it away from him and stabbed him in the skull above the right eye.

It is an account of a remarkable fight, for it is rare for anyone to survive a knife or dagger attack from the rear, disarm the attacker, and turn the blade on him, although it does happen. Indeed, lacking a martial arts background, many academics and writers have refused to accept the truth of the Marlowe story. These critics view the report as a cover story for cold-blooded murder.[12]

But if it was a lie, it was a skillful one, crafted to appeal to the understanding of the common men of the jury. For we know today that the ability to disarm a dagger-wielding man was not so rare a thing after all during the late Middle Ages and early Renaissance. In fact, the techniques of dagger fighting, dagger defense, and dagger taking were then taught across Europe by masters of defense as they had been for centuries. These techniques formed a part of the fighting curriculum of both the knight and the common man, a body of sophisticated knowledge of weapons use and combat as good and as deep as that practiced anywhere in the world. It is likely that the jury in the Marlowe case would have had some familiarity with these methods if they did not practice themselves. So a story couched in terms of those methods, if a lie, contained seeds of the truth—a different truth perhaps than about the circumstances of Marlowe's death—but truth nonetheless.

It is even possible today, knowing what is now known about medieval and Renaissance dagger fighting, to reconstruct the probable events of the fight—or at least the events as described and perhaps even acted out for the coroner's jury by the men who left that upstairs room in Mistress Bull's house alive.

Assume that both men were right-handed. Marlowe approached Frizer from behind. Frizer probably heard him coming and perhaps turned his head. Marlowe snatched Frizer's dagger from its scabbard, or perhaps used his own. Frizer turned and rose as Marlowe lifted his hand to strike, holding the dagger in an icepick grip. Frizer raised his own hands to catch the dagger arm, for grasping the attacking arm is the primary method taught for dagger defense. He was not immediately successful but was able to ward Marlowe's blows enough that he suffered only superficial wounds. (That Frizer suffered two head wounds must be true; the jury would have seen them at the inquest.) Marlowe continued striking; in knife attacks it is common for the attacker to deliver multiple blows until the victim is dead. Marlowe struck altogether three times, two causing Frizer's wounds, but on the third blow, Frizer succeeded in grasping Marlowe's arm. Most likely, Frizer obtained a hold on Marlowe's arm at or just behind the wrist. Frizer used his left hand, although he could have used both; single- and two-handed methods of securing the arm were widely taught. If Frizer used just his left hand, there were two ways to make the grip: on the inside of the arm with the thumb toward the elbow, or on the outside of the arm with the thumb toward Marlowe's hand. Once Frizer had Marlowe's arm, he had only one realistic reply—to take Marlowe's dagger from him. He could not move, according to the testimony, which might have enabled him to lock Marlowe's elbow, so taking the dagger was his only practical alternative. Dagger taking is simple, and Frizer most likely applied the straightforward method of grasping the blade with his right hand and rotating the point toward Marlowe's elbow. Using this

method, a dagger will slip out of the strongest grip. It seems likely that Frizer disarmed Marlowe in this way (or said he did) because of the location of Marlowe's death wound, on the right side of his head above the right eye. Such a wound most likely was inflicted with a left-handed, icepick-style blow. This is exactly the blow that naturally follows a disarm using the right hand on the blade and rotating the point to the elbow. Frizer transferred the dagger to his left hand after stripping it from Marlowe and struck a single downward blow, which penetrated Marlowe's skull and killed him. As improbable a death wound as it may seem, such wounds were not unknown during this period. The London coroners' rolls for the 14th century record several dagger homicides resulting from stabs through the skull.

LESSONS FROM THE PAST

Daggers on the belts of virtually every man in medieval and Renaissance Europe created the imminent risk that they would be used in moments of hot temper, not just in knightly combat or on the battlefield, as the coroners rolls clearly show. Facing such a risk, it is natural that men would invent ways to confront the threat, and medieval and Renaissance men were no exception.

We know that they fashioned solutions for the problem of dagger attack because they wrote books that included advice for dagger fighting.

Many of these books have survived. A few are available for our examination and study today. From these books we can reconstruct the techniques taught and used across Europe for at least two centuries—techniques that probably are far, far older than our oldest source, and are as sophisticated and effective as those used anywhere in the world.

Let us now turn to those sources.

ENDNOTES

1. Konrad Spindler. *The Man in the Ice*. New York: Crown, 1994, pp. 101–103.
2. Xenophon, Betty Radice and Robert Baldick, ed. *The Persian Expedition*. Baltimore: Penguin, 1965, pp. 141–142.
3. Else Roesdahl. *The Vikings*. London: Penguin, 1987), pp. 154–155. One find in Birka, Sweden, contained a knife with the blade almost as long as the man's forearm, as well as a short utility knife.
4. William Short, trans. *The Eyrbriggja Saga* ch. 58, excerpt at www.hurstwic.org/library/ arms_in_sagas.
5. Wrestling in the saddle apparently was common, and many Medieval fight books contain advice on what to do in that situation. See for example Hans Talhoffer, *Medieval Combat*, Mark Rector trans. Mechanicsburg, PA: Greenhill Books, 2000, plates 261–264.
6. Roger Vercel. *Bertrand of Brittany*. New Haven: Yale University Press, 1934, pp. 50–53. For a different version of the fight see Stephen Turnbull. *The Knight Triumphant* London: Cassell & Co., 2001, p. 79. According to Turnbull's version, Guesclin beat Thomas with his mailed fist, not with the pommel of his dagger.
7. Undoubtedly half-swording, a manner of wielding a sword with one hand on the blade and the other on the grip, often used for stabbing.
8. The account and the quotations are taken from Eric Jager. *The Last Duel*. New York: Broadway Books, 2004, pp. 169–179.
9. Reginald R. Sharpe, ed. *Calendar of Coroners Rolls of the City of London A.D. 1300–1378*. Suffolk, England: Richard Clay and Sons, 1913, p. 112.
10. Ibid. p. 129.
11. A.D. Wright and Virginia Stern. *In Search of Christopher Marlowe*. New York: Vanguard Press, 1965, pp. 292–293.
12. Charles Nicholl. *The Reckoning: The Murder of Christopher Marlowe*. New York: Harcourt Brace & Co., 1992.

CHAPTER 2

FECHTBUCHER: WINDOW INTO THE PAST

In an early chapter of James Clavell's *Shogun*, the Englishman, Blackthorne, and his Dutch shipmates are confined in a pit, captives of samurai after their shipwreck. The trapdoor above the prisoners' heads opens, and a samurai orders one of them out. Knowing the man is being called to his death, the prisoners refuse; when the samurai try to force one out, the rest fight back in a futile, ultimately losing battle. Pressing the samurai back temporarily, Blackthorne, armed with a captured dagger, mounts the ladder leading out of the pit in an effort to break out. But at the top, Blackthorne finds two swordsmen waiting with drawn weapons. "Blackthorne knew his dagger was useless against the swords," but he charges up the ladder nonetheless, trying to break out, and is sent reeling back into the pit by a kick to the head. In moments, three dagger-armed samurai leap into the pit and drive the helpless, frightened prisoners back, taking one of them to be tortured to death. Bitter at the defeat, Blackthorne wishes he had the same skill in close combat that he had painfully experienced earlier at the hands of a Japanese villager.[1]

It makes for a good story, but at its foundation is the persistent myth that the Europeans of the time were inept at close combat. In reality, while a properly trained European fighter in the *Shogun* period would have known he was in desperate trouble facing swordsmen while only armed with a dagger, he would not have felt the dagger was utterly useless. Medieval and Renaissance Europeans practiced dagger-to-sword combat and knew what to do even when unarmed and facing weapons.

The foundations for this myth were laid in the 19th century by sport fencers, who proclaimed that their methods of foil-based fencing were the pinnacle of progress in the combat arts. They maintained that their fencing was graceful, elegant, and, more importantly, modern. Necessarily, all that had come before in Europe involved brutish, crude, inartful, unsophisticated hacking and slashing.[2] Subsequent writers and historians, who knew nothing about close combat of the period, have accepted this verdict uncritically. In discussing medieval European dagger fights, for instance, the otherwise well-informed

9

blade historian Harold Peterson opined, "Strength rather than skill normally prevailed."[3] The view is so prevalent in many circles that it is now received wisdom that is often hard, if not impossible, to dispel. Clavell and others in the West have merely built upon this edifice to suppose that the samurai were invincible and that no European could ever have stood against them.

But now we know that this assessment is false. The record disproves it. Medieval and Renaissance combat in all spheres before the advent of the rapier, the celebrated ancestor of the foil, was highly sophisticated and required a great deal of skill. We know because the old masters left detailed instructions on their methods in writing.

THE MASTERS' WORDS

Despite the depredations of time, there are scores of such manuals on the shelves of museums, libraries, and private collections that are worthy of study.[4] Indeed, the masters of the medieval and Renaissance periods, especially the Germans, were "compulsive compilers of combat manuals."[5] The books vary in quality and in manner of presentation: Some contain drawings with only a small amount of often cryptic text; others have pictures and more text; still others are nothing but text. But regardless of how they present the material, all are illuminating. Some are extraordinary.

More and more of these books, known collectively as fight books or *fechtbucher*, are coming to light. A number have been translated into English and are available to a wide audience either through book publication or on the Internet. More become available with each passing year. Most are not step-by-step, how-to books detailing a fighting system from the ground up, but rather they generally seem more intended as memory aids to assist a student already familiar with the fundamentals and the

techniques. Despite that limitation and the secretive nature of some of the books, it is possible to decipher them and reconstruct the nature of medieval and Renaissance combat methods.

These manuals have a lot to say about close combat because they are often all-inclusive, addressing mounted combat, swordplay, the spear, the staff, wrestling, dagger play, fighting in armor and without, and more—in short, the entire curriculum for the well-rounded warrior. "The masters taught everything that pertained to physical violence in times of peace and war. They dealt with every weapon and every trick of unarmed combat."[6]

Let's take a moment to survey the field and see something of what's out there. The oldest known European martial arts manual, the *I.33* manuscript, which deals with sword-and-buckler combat, dates from about 1300. Apparently written in Germany, the manuscript is now at the Royal Armouries in Britain. It is a beautiful book. The pictures are rendered in color, and the manual depicts, with its Latin text, an efficient method of single combat.

In the mid-1300s, Johannes Liechtenauer began teaching his method of combat in Germany. Liechtenauer was probably born in Liechtenau, Franconia, circa 1320. We know very little about his life—as we know very little about the lives of most of the authors of the fight books. He apparently traveled throughout the Holy Roman Empire and Eastern Europe, learning swordsmanship and gradually incorporating what he had learned into his own system. His, like that of other masters, was a broad, integrated combat system, which included use of the lance, the sword, wrestling, and the dagger.[7] He taught these weapons for use in harness (in armor) and without. He also taught mounted combat. Liechtenauer left a written record of his teachings in a collection of terse, often cryptic verses. Nonetheless, Liechtenauer was the most significant German medieval swordsman. He influenced generations of German swordsmen, and his methods were widely emulated and passed on.

In 1389 one of Liechtenauer's students, a priest named Hanko Döbringer, wrote a lengthy commentary on his master's method and others, such as Sigmund Ringeck in about 1420, attempted interpretations. Liechtenauer is thought to have inspired many additional figures in medieval and Renaissance combat, such as Paulus Kal, Peter Falkner, Hans von Speyer, Ludwig von Eyb, Gregor Erhart, Sigmund Schining, Andre Pauernfeindt, and more.[8]

Also producing treatises in the mid-1400s in Germany was Hans Talhoffer, whose work appeared in at least three editions.

German masters continued to produce manuscripts into the 1500s. Some were independent works, such as Joachim Meyer's extraordinary book in 1570, which is illustrated by wonderfully clear text and detailed woodcuts, and Hans Wurm's wrestling book. Fabian von Auerswald's 1538 wrestling treatise shows many locks and throws similar to those found in modern judo. Paulus Hector Mair put together an immense, well-illustrated manual in about 1540 covering longsword, dagger, the staff, wrestling, and other weapons, some of them quite exotic. Others were collections by anonymous authors, such as the beautiful and detailed *Codex Wallerstein*, which appeared in the mid-1400s. Some were derivative, copies of earlier works. For instance, it is thought that Renaissance artist Albrecht Dürer's fight book is a copy of the *Codex Wallerstein* (although its artwork is far superior to the *Codex's*, not surprising since Dürer was a master artist). The Solothurner fight book is thought by some modern scholars to be a copy of Paulus Kal's work.

The Germans were not the only nation to produce a crop of fight books. The Italians were busy throughout the medieval and Renaissance periods as well. In 1409 an Italian knight named Fiore dei Liberi produced the *Flos Duellatorum*, the first known Italian manual and in many ways one of the best in Europe. By about 1450, Filippo Vadi published his *Arte Gladiatoria Dimicandi*, which some modern scholars think is heavily influenced by Fiore's work. In the 1480s a Spanish knight living in Italy, Pietro Monte, wrote extensively on all manner of personal combat. In the 1500s Achille Marozzo published the influential *Opera Nova*. (He found a critic in the Florentine master Francesco Altoni, who disputed many of Marozzo's views.) Angelo Viggianni's 1551 work *Lo Schermo* introduced use of a longer, more slender sword to be used one-handed, as the transition to the rapier began. Camillo Agrippa's 1553 manual favored the thrust over the cut in duelling as the evolution to the rapier continued, ultimately culminating in major rapier works by Giacomo Di Grassi and Vincentio Saviolo.

Spain produced its own manuals. One of the most notable was by Juan Quixada de Reayo in 1548 dealing with mounted combat. Pedro Heredia's rapier manual from about 1600 combines grappling and throwing with the use of that long, thrusting blade similar to methods propounded by Fiore in 1409.

The Dutch were late to publish manuals, but some of them have been significant. Nicolaes Petter's 1674 *Clear Instructions to the Excellent Art of Wrestling* is considered by author Sydney Anglo to be the best period work on the subject.[9]

The French, however, do not seem to have been inclined to commit details of their combat arts to writing. Only one French manual from the period is known, and it dealt with the pole ax.

Saviolo's work was published in English, and his teachings and those of other Italian rapier fencers in London provoked a major reaction in England. George Silver's influential works in part were an attack on rapier fencing and a defense of older cut-and-thrust methods.

This recitation of some of the major works is

hardly exhaustive. There are far more fine manuals in existence that we can address here.[10] That the public does not know more about them is unfortunate. I merely hope to give the reader some idea of the energy expended on recording European combat arts and illustrate the fact that the practice of these arts was widespread throughout the continent. The existence of these works also shows that the roots of European swordsmanship are both old, organized, and accomplished. In contrast, Japanese kenjutsu did not begin to form into styles, or systematized methods of practice and the transmission of information, until after 1500.[11]

SOURCES FOR THIS BOOK

The techniques that follow in subsequent chapters do not draw on all the sources mentioned above—there are far too many manuals for that. Sydney Anglo claims that there were at least 56 German period manuals that address wrestling and/or dagger fighting.[12] Rather, these chapters offer interpretations of techniques contained in a selected sample of manuals. Nor do they contain all the techniques in this sample. The aim is to convey core techniques and the principles behind them so that the reader has an appreciation for the richness and sophistication of this European combat art, the art of the dagger. Taken together, the manuals "comprise a consistent and formidable system."[13]

Thus, the primary sources for this work are Fiore dei Liberi's *Flos Duellatorum*, Hans Talhoffer's fechtbucher, Filippo Vadi's *Arte Gladiatoria Dimicandi*, the *Gladiatoria*, Achille Marozzo, Hans Cynner, the *Codex Wallerstein*, Albrecht Durer, Joachim Meyer, George Silver, and Paulus Kal and the Solothurner fechtbucher.

Fiore dei Liberi's *Flos Duellatorum*
The manual was written about 1409 and exists in three known versions: the Getty, the Pisani-Dossi, and the Morgan. The Getty is held by the Getty Museum in Los Angeles. The Pisani-Dossi is known only through a transcription done in the late 19th century (however, it has been reported that the original manuscript has been found in a private collection). The Morgan is held by the Pierpont Morgan Library in New York City. While there are often significant variations among the versions between the text and the ordering of the material, it is one of today's principal and most accessible sources for medieval combat technique. Fiore's manual covers all aspects of medieval and early Renaissance combat: the longsword, pole arms, mounted combat, and combat wrestling, as well as dagger combat. Although today we associate swordplay with men of the medieval and Renaissance periods, combat involving the dagger predominated Fiore's manual. Of 287 images in the *Flos*, 99 dealt with some form of dagger combat.[14]

As far as dagger combat goes, the *Flos* is most valuable for its systematic treatment of unarmed dagger defense. Fiore's method of description is extraordinarily well organized, divided into sections of related techniques. Each section begins with a cover and an interception of the attacker's arm, followed with all the techniques that were available after having performed that cover. (This book is patterned after his approach.) Fiore is also one of the few to illustrate techniques for dagger-vs.-sword combat.

Fiore is unique among the old masters in that probably more is known about him and his career than anyone else. Most of these biographical details come from the various prologues or introductions to the *Flos*. Fiore says he was the son of Benedetto dei Liberi, a minor gentryman holding land near the northeastern Italian village of Premariacco in Friuli. No fixed date is given for his birth, but it is estimated to be around 1350. Fiore tells us that from his boyhood he aspired to learn martial arts. To achieve his ambition, he says he traveled widely (although he does not say where), and he learned from German and Italian masters. Because we do not know where he traveled, we cannot be sure that he went to Germany, but there are similarities between both his sword fencing methods and his wrestling to those taught by Germans like Hans Talhoffer. He evidently gained a considerable reputation and "the said Fiore was more and more times required by many Gentleman and Knights and Squires for learning from the said Fiore [the] art of all arms and armour and fighting in the barriers to the death which art he has demonstrated to more Italian and German and other great Gentlemen who had to fight in the barriers."[15]

In the Getty and Pisani-Dossi introductions, Fiore identifies many of his students who fought in the barriers and their opponents—one of whom apparently included a future marshal of France, who was defeated twice by Fiore's students. Fiore himself fought five sword duels without armor (apparently victoriously, as he claims to have emerged unscathed). There is evidence that he also fought in the constant wars occurring throughout northern Italy during the late 14th century.[16]

Around 1400, Fiore took service with Niccolo d'Este, the marquis of Ferrara and lord of Parma. Because "without books no one shall be a good Master nor Scholar in this art," Fiore determined to set down what he knew.[17] "And I, Fiore, confirm it true that this art is long that there is no man of the world of great memory that he can hold in his mind without books a quarter part of this art."[18] At this time, Fiore said he had studied martial arts for more than 40 years (and even then he felt "I am not a very perfect Master in this art," although others thought him to be one).[19] Out of his ambition grew the versions of the manuals we have today.

The date of his death is not known.

Hans Talhoffer's fechtbucher

Talhoffer was born about 1420 and died about 1490. He was the master at arms for Leutold von Königsegg, a Swabian knight.[20]

Talhoffer's work is available in three known versions published under his name, the 1443, the 1459, and the 1467 editions. The 1467 edition has been translated by Mark Rector and published under the name *Medieval Combat*. Portions of the 1459 version have been translated by Brian Hunt. The original 1467 edition consists of 320 images of individual techniques involving armored and unarmored longsword play, the messer (a swordlike long knife), the pole axe, judicial combat with oddly shaped shields, sword-and-buckler and mounted fighting—all vividly rendered in color. About 42 of these images illustrate dagger techniques.

His portrait is included on the last plate of the 1467 edition.[21]

Filippo Vadi's *Arte Gladiatoria Dimicandi*

Filippo Vadi was a Pisan. He learned his fencing "through practical experience and doctrine from many masters in various and different countries."[22] He dedicated the work to the duke of Urbino, Guidobaldo da Montefeltro.

The *Arte Gladiatoria* dates from 1482–1485. This work is available in English translation. Despite Vadi's claim that he had traveled widely and learned from various masters, his method is considered derivative of Fiore. Although the treatise focuses on the sword, a significant proportion is devoted to the dagger work. He depicts 34 techniques involving the dagger, 23 of them unarmed against that weapon. Twenty-five of these techniques are identical to those found in Fiore's work.[23] However, some of Vadi's material differs from Fiore's and is worthy of independent examination.

Alone of the masters, he describes the perfect length of the dagger.

The *Gladiatoria*

An anonymous German fight book created in the mid-1400s, the *Gladiatoria* depicts fighting armor with a variety of weapons, including the dagger. There are 36 standing dagger techniques depicted and seven pinning techniques on the ground. Dr. Jeffrey Forgeng of the Higgins Museum in Worcester, Massachusetts, has translated the dagger portions of this manuscript.

Achille Marozzo

Achille Marozzo was an Italian who published the combat treatise known as the *Opera Nova* in 1536. It was a very popular and influential work that was reprinted three times in the 1500s and at least once in the 1600s.[24]

By Marozzo's time, unarmed or dagger combat was not taught as the centerpiece or foundation of close combat, as it had been in Fiore's day. Most Italian masters of the mid-1500s relegated dagger and unarmed play to an appendage of the curriculum, if such techniques were taught at all.[25] Thus, Marozzo's focus was largely on the sword, with some additional instruction on the dagger, although he considered the ability to defend against a dagger attack "necessary for men in those times 'for the conservation of their life.'"[26] In the last book of the *Opera* there were only 22 techniques for the unarmed man facing a dagger.[27]

Hans Cynner

Cynner was a German who wrote in the 1400s. I have not found a translation of Cynner yet. The work covers combat in armor with both sword and dagger. His work is notable because it illustrates dagger and sword defenses involving locks to the off arm (the non-weapon-bearing arm).

The *Codex Wallerstein*

The *Codex* is a hand-drawn and lettered manuscript of armored and unarmed fighting with various weapons and unarmed combat.[28] It is apparently a collection of material by several different artists and writers, and depicts methods in use in Germany during the late 14th or early 15th centuries. The manuscript was once owned by the martial artist Paulus Hector Mair, a prodigious collector and author of martial arts manuals who was hanged for embezzling money to support his collection. This major work has been translated by Grzegorz Zabinski and Bartlomiej Walczak. It shows 14 techniques for unarmed dagger fighting and nine for armored dagger fighting.

Albrecht Durer

Durer was the celebrated German realist artist. It is not widely known, however, that he also produced a martial arts book in 1512 that included aspects of dagger fighting. He apparently was a fencer himself, for he was a member of a German fencing association, the Brotherhood of St. Mark.[29] Despite its skillfully rendered illustrations, the work is considered by well-known martial arts author Sydney Anglo to be largely a copy of the *Codex Wallerstein*.[30] This assessment is not completely fair, however, because Durer's book contains material not found in the *Codex*, such as dagger defenses against a sword attack.

Joachim Meyer

A citizen of the free city of Strasbourg, Joachim Meyer, an ethnic German, wrote one of the most sophisticated Renaissance fight books in existence, the beautifully illustrated and lucid *Kunst des Fechtens (Art of Fighting)*, published in 1570. Although many fight masters directed their teachings to members of the knightly class, other masters were commoners who taught combat arts to their fellows. By the 1500s, there were many such commoner instructors and whole societies, or brotherhoods, devoted to the study and practice of martial arts. Meyer was a freifechter, or free fighter, however, who is not known to have belonged to any such brotherhood.

Meyer's manual is an extraordinary collection of advice about all manner of period combat, including the sword, staff, wrestling, and the dagger. His manual was so popular that it underwent several reprintings following its first appearance. Dr. Jeffrey Forgeng has translated the dagger portion of this work, which Sydney Anglo considers to be very important.[31]

George Silver

Silver was an Englishman who wrote two important martial arts manuals around 1600, *Paradoxes of Defence* and a follow-up called *The Brief Instructions on my Paradoxes of Defence*. The first was published in 1598, while the latter remained unpublished and unknown until 1898. These two brief books are must-reads for any martial artist, regardless of his or her discipline. They describe universal principles of time, place, and distance that are shared by all close-combat arts, including the dagger. Mark Hillyard provides an excellent analysis of Silver's principles in *Master of Defence: The Works of George Silver*, Paul Wagner ed.

The *Brief Instructions* is of interest because it describes the relative advantages of various weapons when matched against each other. As part of this discussion, the *Brief Instructions* contains advice on the dagger-to-dagger fight. Its main drawback is that it does not describe specific techniques for use in such an encounter, but rather sets out underlying principles and considerations for that fight.

Paulus Kal and the Solothurner fechtbuch

Paulus Kal was a fight master who served a Bavarian duke from 1458 to 1467. Generally considered to be in the Liechtenauer tradition, he produced a fight book in about 1460 that includes aspects of dagger combat.

The Solothurner fechtbuch is an anonymous work produced about 1500. Considered by some to be a copy of Kal, it is named for the town where it was found, Solothurn, Switzerland.

ENDNOTES

1. James Clavell. *Shogun.* New York: Dell, 1975, pp. 80–85.
2. See:
   Sydney Anglo, *The Martial Arts of Renaissance Europe* (New Haven: Yale University Press, 2000), p. 103;
   John Clements. *Top Myths of Renaissance Martial Arts.* Association for Renaissance Martial Arts, http://www.thearma.org/essays/TopMyths.htm, undated;
   John Clements. *The Art of Well Meaning Error.* Association for Renaissance Martial Arts, http://www.thearma.org/essays/barbasetti.htm, undated;
   Christoph J. Amberger. *The Secret History of the Sword.* Burbank, CA: Unique Publications, 1996, pp. 135–136.
3. Harold Peterson. *Daggers and Fighting Knives of the Western World.* New York: Walker and Co., p. 12.
4. There are at least 70 surviving fighting manuals from the 14th to early 17th centuries in German alone. Anglo, p. 181.
5. Ibid., p. 109.
6. Ibid., p. 37.
7. The primary blade weapon of Liechtenauer's system, as in most other period systems, was what we today call the longsword, a weapon about 48 inches from point to pommel, with about 36 inches of blade, on the average. Contrary to many modern interpretations (especially from Hollywood), a longsword was not a cumbersome weapon, but rather was light and quick—an elegant weapon in the hands of an experienced fighter. It was

capable of being wielded with one or two hands, although it was usually held in both hands, to thrust and to cut. It first made its appearance in Europe during the mid-1200s.

8. "Renaissance Martial Arts Literature," www.thearma.org/RMAlit.htm. Tobler adds, "The *fechtbucher* of this period (14th through 17th centuries) often begin with a complete recitation of Liechtenauer's verse, followed by passages quoting specific *merk-verse* couplets together with the explanatory glosa." Christian Henry Tobler. *Secrets of German Medieval Swordsmanship: Sigmund Ringeck's Commentaries on Master Liechtenauer's Verse.* Chivalry Bookshelf, 2001, p. X.

9. Anglo, p. 192.

10. Anglo is the best source for discovering the wealth of material that is available on medieval and Renaissance combat. Arthur Wise's *Art and History of Personal Combat* is another good source for general information.

11. Hiraoki Sato. *The Sword & the Mind.* New York: Barnes & Noble Books, 2004, p. 12.

12. Anglo, p. 181.

13. Ibid., p. 181.

15. Ibid., p 177. The breakdown, according to Anglo's analysis, is as follows:
> 20 illustrations involving wrestling.
> 90 involving unarmed combat against the knife or knife-to-knife.
> 60 involving the longsword.
> 18 involving the one-hand sword.
> 22 involving the longsword in armored combat.
> 16 involving the ax.
> 5 involving the spear and staff.

> 9 involving the dagger against the sword.
> 43 involving mounted combat.

15. Fiore dei Liberi. *Flos Duellatorum*, Getty MS (1409). Rob Lovett, Mark Davidson and Mark Lancaster, trans. http://forie.the-exiles.org/G-introduction.html.

16. Matt Easton, untitled biography of Fiore dei Liberi. www.fioredeiliberi.org/fiore/

17. Fiore, Getty MS.

18. Ibid.

19. Ibid. Fiore's humility contrasts sharply with the egoism so prevalent in the martial arts today.

20. Hans Talhoffer, Mark Rector trans., *Medieval Combat.* Mechanicsburg, PA: Greenhill Books, 2000, p. 9.

21. Rector, plate 270.

22. Filippo Vadi. *Arte Gladiatoria Dimicandi.* Luca Porzio and Gregory Mele transl. Union City, CA: Chivalry Bookshelf, 2002, p. 4.

23. Ibid., p. 9.

24. Anglo, p. 135.

25. Vadi, p. 9.

26. Anglo, p. 187.

27. Anglo, p. 137.

28. Of interest, unlike many other manuals, the *Codex Wallerstein* has at least 10 methods for defending against the fist punch, including a front kick to the groin or stomach to stop hit the punch. See:
The Codex Wallerstein. Grzegorz Zabinski and Bartolomeij Walczak, transl. Boulder, CO: Paladin Press, 2002, plate 134.

29. Talhoffer, p. 11.

30. Anglo, p. 183–184.

31. Ibid., p. 190.

CHAPTER 3

FORMS OF THE DAGGER

A study of armed combat can't occur without some appreciation for the characteristics of the weapons involved, as form dictates how the weapon is used. Daggers and knives are not swords, and their shorter length requires combat techniques that are unlike those used in swordplay.

The general form and function of combat daggers and knives have remained relatively constant since their invention, which may have taken place more than 200,000 years ago. They all have a point for stabbing and often one or two edges. But even so, there has been a great deal of variation in dagger design over the millennia. By the medieval and Renaissance periods, there were an enormous number of different types. The London coroner's rolls for 1300–1378 record homicides by weapons with bewildering names: bideu, trenchour (a type of carving knife), the Irish knife, the thwytel, the anelace, the bazelard (or baselard), poinard, and the misericorde, among others.

Scandinavian sources mention a "bear knife," although it is not clear what it looked like. Also mentioned are assaults with other types of impromptu cutting and stabbing weapons, such as the tools used in leather work.

Because of this proliferation of types, it is difficult to generalize about the forms of the medieval and Renaissance dagger, just as it is hard to generalize about combat knives today. The most that can be said is that they can be grouped into broad categories based on the general form of the grip and the blade. But even within those categories, there is a great deal of variation. For instance, the rondel, identifiable by its round hilt and pommel disks, was predominantly used for thrusting. This, plus the fact many manuals describe dagger-taking methods involving blade grabbing, has led some people to conclude that the rondel (and by extension many other medieval and Renaissance daggers) lacked a useful edge. But that would be wrong. Some rondels had edges. Many other medieval and Renaissance dagger types had edges too. Some did not. Care must be taken when making broad claims about these weapons.

SAX

The sax was the signature blade of the Germanic peoples. It was so widely carried by Germans and Franks that it may have given its name to a tribe, the Saxons, who populated England and have a German state named for them. The sax is also called a scramasax, a name derived from a reference in Gregory of Tour's history of the Franks, who mentioned "boys with strong knives which they commonly call *scramasaxos*."[1] It was a highly popular design and was in use longer than any other in Western Europe during the Dark Ages and medieval period. It appeared in the 8th century, and versions were still being made in England in the late 15th century.

The blade enjoyed such long and widespread use because of its versatility. The design lent itself to use both as a weapon and as a common tool. It was a working knife carried by people at all levels of society, both rich and poor.

Sax.

Saxes could be elegant in appearance. They ranged in length from 3.5 inches to as much as 30 inches, intruding into sword length at that point. In form, they were single-edged. The long and short edges ran parallel from the grip, with the back often driving straight to the point and the edge clipping sharply downward to meet it or dipping to the point in a great curve. However, some edges curved slightly to meet the point. The cross section was triangular, narrowing from a "thick and robust" back to the long edge side of the blade.[2] Tangs extended the length of the grip. "Hilts were generally formed with semicircular wooden cheek plates riveted to the tang sides then bound with leather and wire."[3]

Pommels apparently were small and not elaborately designed.

Remarkably, a few sheaths have survived. Some were a folded strip of leather, often riveted to close the open edge of the fold. Others were made of wooden slats. These scabbards could be suspended from a belt by metal rings or leather thongs, or simply thrust into it.

PEASANT KNIFE

The sax evolved into the peasant knife. It got this name because mainly villagers and peasants, men and women alike, carried it. Most surviving examples are German, and German commentators have dubbed it the *hauswehre*, or home weapon.[4]

In form, the tool tended to resemble a modern butcher or kitchen knife. The blade ran parallel from the cross or hilt, with the long edge curving up to the point. However, some designs were very saxlike, with the back and long edge curving to meet each other. Other versions of these weapons had clipped points, giving them a striking resemblance to the American Bowie knife. Still others had triangular shaped blades, long and slender in form, although these too were single-edged.[5]

The design of this weapon indicates that it was intended primarily as a general utility blade and secondarily as a weapon. Perhaps the "Irish knife" mentioned in the London coroner's rolls was such a blade.

Peasant knife.

QUILLON DAGGER

Throughout the medieval and Renaissance period, a form now called the quillon dagger was in widespread use. This dagger was marked by the presence of a crossbar, or quillon, at the base of the blade. Thompson claims that this type of dagger was a small copy of the sword.[6] Blades were "slender, narrow, double-edged, slightly diamond" shaped in cross section, tapering slightly to the point.[7] Pommels varied in design. Some were round. Some were rings. Many attempted to copy the enormous variety of sword pommels in existence. Apparently, swords and daggers might be made in matched sets. Other quillon daggers had crescent-shaped pommel bars, much like an ancient Celtic design known today as the "antenna" dagger for the pommels' weird resemblance to the old V-shaped TV antenna.

Quillon daggers were regarded as military rather than civilian weapons and were carried mainly by knights and soldiers.[8] As such, they were originally intended to be deployed when the sword was no longer available. With their double edges, they are the classic form that the word "dagger" brings to the modern mind.

At the opening of the Renaissance, the quillons of these weapons grew in length and the base acquired a thumb ring as the weapon evolved into a secondary arm used in conjunction with the cut-and-thrust sword and the rapier.[9]

RONDEL

Rondel is the name given to a diverse group of weapons that share one common characteristic: a disc-shaped hilt. The name is modern. The French called this weapon a *dague a rouelle* and the Germans called it a *scheibendolch*.[10]

This very popular dagger appeared perhaps as early as 1300 or even slightly before, and by 1325 was in general use, spreading from Scandinavia in the north to Spain in the south, and Britain in the west to as far east as Poland—in short, throughout western and central Europe.[11] Variations of the design, going through many modifications but still carrying the disc-shaped or round hilt, continued in use until about 1550, although the wooden dagger wasters in Joachim Meyer's fechtbuch (1570) appear to be modeled on rondels.[12]

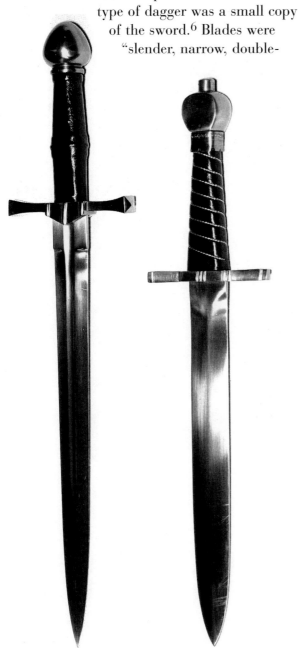

Examples of modern reproductions of quillon daggers.

The hilt rather than the blade design defined the weapon. It was disc-shaped, sometimes round, sometimes discoidal, sometimes octagonal or hexagonal. Thickness of the hilt varied. Some were quite thin, others were thick and robust. In early incarnations, the pommel was not a disc, but often wheel-shaped, "spherical, conical, or onion-shaped."[13] However, by about 1400 the pommel came to resemble the hilt, assuming a discoidal or round form. After 1450, the fashion in rondels was for very large hilt and pommel discs "(so) that it is almost impossible to hold the weapon in anything but a stabbing grip, with the wide pommel above the thumb."[14]

The grip tended to be simple and cylindrical with straight sides, although as time went on the grip sometimes assumed a barrel shape.

Blade designs varied a great deal and there was apparently no standard version. As a general rule, the blades were "straight, slender, tapering," and triangular in silhouette, and could be "either single- or double-edged."[15] By about 1400, the rondel blade was generally short, double-edged, and diamond-shaped in cross section. During the following century, the blade grew in length and slenderness and was as often single- as double-edged.[16] The diamond cross section was not the only form. I have handled a period rondel whose blade was triangular in cross section, and some surviving versions resemble little more than spikes with grips.[17]

This was a military rather than civilian weapon and was carried predominantly by knights and soldiers. Its popularity with the military class probably arose from its ability to pierce mail. The rondel rose to prominence during the period when plate began to replace mail as the primary body armor, but mail never completely disappeared from the knightly panoply. There were gaps in plate at the joints and these places, especially at the neck, shoulder, armpit, and the groin, remained protected by mail. Test-cutting experiments with narrow sword blades

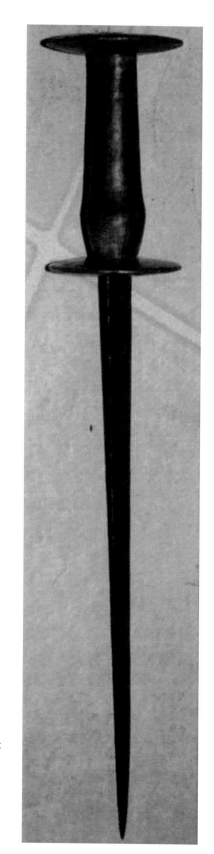

Above: Modern reproduction rondel.

Right: An authentic rondel from the collection of Hank Reinhardt. Photo courtesy of John Clements.

20

that resemble rondel blades show that relatively narrow blades will penetrate mail. So the soldier or knight most likely used the rondel to thrust through the gaps in the plates, hoping to pierce any mail or gambeson filling the gap. Contemporary artwork, such as that found in Talhoffer (1459) and the *Gladiatoria* (1450), shows the use of a rondel to attack the neck of a fallen knight.

BASELARD

In the late 13th century, another dagger design arose to rival the rondel in popularity. This was the baselard, so named for the city of its probable but unknown inventor, Basel, Switzerland. Members of this dagger family were more widely used than the rondel, for it was considered both a military and civilian arm. "People from all walks of life carried baselards."[18] It was popular with Italians as well as southern German knights, and was widely carried in England. An English poem from the period illustrates the arm's popularity in that country:

There is no man worth a leke,
Be he sturdy, be he meke,
But he bear a basilard.[19]

By the late 15th century, however, knights ceased to carry the arm, and it became an exclusively civilian weapon.

Like the rondel, the defining characteristic of the baselard was its hilt and pommel. These were surprisingly uniform, shaped like an "I", the base of the "I" forming the hilt and the top forming the pommel, although there was considerable variation within this general form. The "I" shape derived from the wooden slats forming the hilt, grip, and pommel, which were riveted to the tang. The lengths of the hilt and pommel varied. Some were short, but others were quite long and appear awkward to handle. Like the

broad hilt and pommel discs of the later rondels, such long pieces on the baselard must have made it easier to use in the reverse grip than the straight grip.

Blades varied less than for rondels. Baselard blades tended to be triangular in silhouette, tapering from the hilt to the point, in form very much like you see for quillon daggers. They were often diamond in cross section and invariably had distinctive edges, usually two, but sometimes one. Some versions had two fullers near the hilt.[20]

BALLOCK DAGGER

The ballock dagger is named for its predominant feature, two lobes that form the hilt and resemble a certain anatomical part. (Whoever invented this form must have had a real sense of humor.) Victorians, unable to say the word ballock, called this weapon a kidney dagger instead.[21] The French called it a *dague a couilettes*.

This dagger first appeared about 1300 and by 1350 had achieved its distinct, well-developed form. It became increasingly common through the end of the 14th century and

Baselard.

remained in use in Europe to the end of the 16th century, still being depicted in Flemish art of the 1550-1560s.[23] In England the ballock dagger remained in use into the 17th century before disappearing, and in Scotland it evolved into the Scottish dirk.[23]

It owed its long survival to its adoption by civilians, for, although the knightly class carried it for a time, it was widely popular with merchants, artisans, and even the poor.

As with other European daggers, the ballock constituted a family of varying designs that shared a distinctive feature, in this case, the lobed hilt. The lobes varied in size, naturally. The blade tended to be more knifelike in that it generally had a single rather than a double edge.

These forms constitute the main, but not the only form of dagger in use in Europe during the Middle Ages and Renaissance. There were other forms as well, including the weird eared dagger with its double flaring earlike pommels, the Holbein, and the cinqueda with its broad triangular blade. However, the daggers described here were the most common and the rondel and ballock predominate in the sources available to

Ballock dagger.

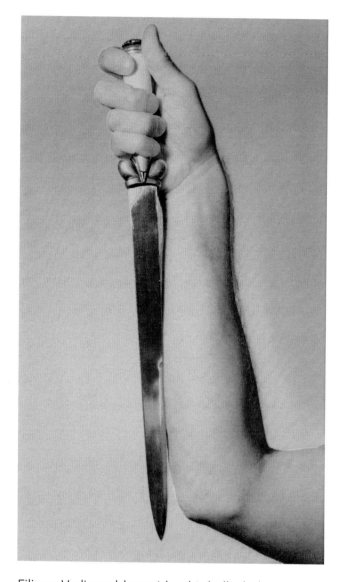

Filippo Vadi would consider this ballock dagger to be of the proper length.

us. These were the primary weapons men trained to fight with and against.

THE IDEAL LENGTH OF THE DAGGER

The length of the medieval and Renaissance dagger varied enormously and there was no set standard. However, Filippo Vadi dared to prescribe a proper length for the dagger. He said the blade should "reach to the elbow."[24] I think he means that when you grip the weapon, its point should reach to the elbow. Vadi did not explain why the dagger should be that size; however, a weapon longer than that begins to approach the sword category and becomes more awkward to use, particularly in the reverse grip. A dagger shorter than that is less effective as a backup weapon against the sword.

The dagger design has stood the test of time. It is a form that is still with us in its many variations.

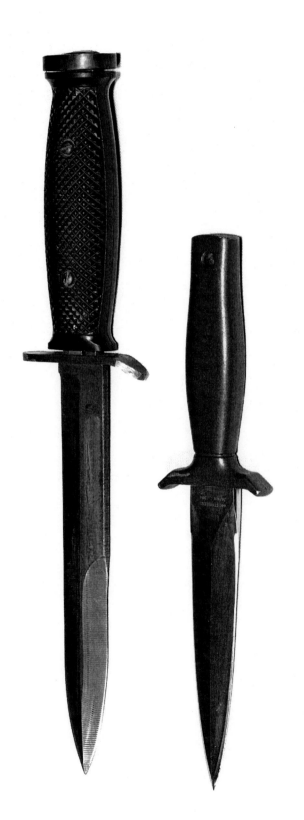

Daggers come in many varieties.

ENDNOTES

1. Logan Thompson. *Daggers and Bayonets: A History*. Boulder, CO: Paladin Press, 1999, p. 15.
2. Ibid., p. 19.
3. Ibid.
4. Harold L. Peterson. *Daggers and Fighting Knives of the Western World: From the Stone Age till 1900*. New York: Walker & Company, 1968, p. 34; Thompson, p. 40.
5. Thompson, p. 23.
6. Ibid., p. 25.
7. Ibid.
8. Peterson, p. 24.
9. Ibid., pp. 30–33.
10. Peterson, p. 13.
11. Ibid., p. 14.
12. Ibid.
13. Ibid.
14. Ibid., p. 15.
15. Thompson, p. 25.
16. Bashford Dean. *Catalogue of European Daggers 1300–1800*. New York: Metropolitan Museum of Art, 1929, p. 39.
17. Thompson, p. 24.
18. Peterson, p. 18.
19. Ibid., p. 19.

20. Thompson, pp. 26–27.

21. Ibid., p. 27; Peterson notes dryly, "Some of the surviving hilts were remarkably phalliform in their contours."

22. Peterson, p. 27.

23. Ibid.

24. Filippo Vadi. *Arte Gladiatoria Dimicandi.* Luca Porzio and Gregory Mele, trans. Union City, CA: Chivalry Bookshelf, 2002, p. 179.

CHAPTER 4

COMMON FUNDAMENTALS

Medieval and Renaissance dagger fighting addressed three core problems of combat: unarmed defense against the dagger, dagger-to-dagger combat, and dagger defense against other weapons, particularly the sword. Each component had different considerations and techniques special to its own area. But there were overlapping concepts common to all of them. These shared features involved the grip on the weapon, how to deliver blows, footwork, covering, and the role played by wrestling.

I will not address how the dagger was carried other than to say that period artwork generally shows it carried on the right side of the body, where it was within quick reach of the dominant hand of most men.[1] The sources on which I have relied do not discuss this topic, so it is beyond the scope of the work, which concerns itself with the narrower question of how the dagger was used or defeated.

GRIP

The sources show two primary ways to grip the dagger: the reverse grip and the forward grip.

Reverse Grip

In the reverse grip, the weapon is grasped with the blade projecting below the little finger in the same manner as you would hold an ice pick.

The reverse grip.

The forward grip.

Infrequently, an alternate reverse grip with the thumb on the pommel is seen.

Forward Grip

In the forward grip, the blade projects above the thumb with the little finger toward the pommel. The thumb is depicted in the sources as locking across the fingers and not along the upper part of the grip, as is fashionable in some modern knife-fighting systems.[2] This grip was apparently Fiore's preferred way to use the dagger "because this gives cover 'from below and above, and every part.'"[3] It is an ancient method for holding the dagger. A Greek vase painting more than 2,500 years old shows the dagger being wielded in this grip to deliver a blow to the stomach.[4]

Regardless of the grip, the weapon could be used for both covering—that is, warding off or redirecting blows and interdicting lines of attack—and for cuts and thrusts. Cuts seem to have been delivered only when employing the forward grip.[5]

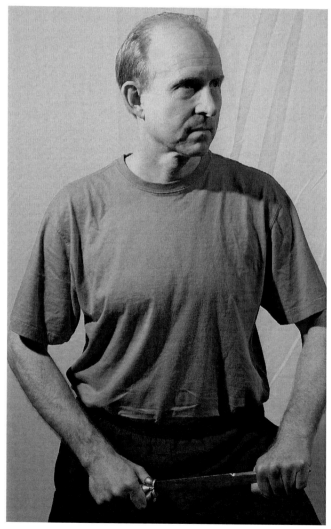

In the forward grip, the dagger was also held in two hands, one on the grip and the other on the blade.

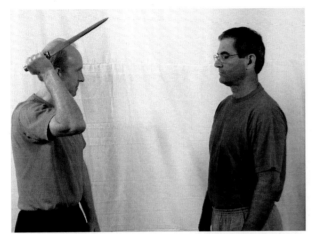

The overhead strike with a reverse grip.

People tend to deliver the overhead blow in a pendulum fashion in practice, a habit that must be vigorously discouraged. All blows in training should be delivered realistically, as they would be in combat.

DELIVERING BLOWS

The primary use of the medieval and Renaissance dagger was to stab rather than cut, according to the sources.

Reverse Grip Blows

There were five blows with the reverse grip: overhead; overhead, diagonal from the right; overhead, diagonal from the left; backhand horizontal; and below.

Overhead

This blow is delivered as if you are hammering a nail. It derives its force from the straightening of the arm or unhinging of your elbow joint. Fiore says this blow is good for attacks from the top of the head to the level of the elbow (about waist level) and not below.[6]

All the manuals depict this type of blow, and it is probable that this was the way that the masters anticipated the dagger would be used most often. The blow can be extremely powerful. The London coroner's rolls record several deaths resulting when the dagger penetrated the victim's skull—the same manner of death suffered by Marlowe. These blows probably were dealt in the reverse grip. However, an icepick-style blow does not have to be delivered with the full force of the arm. Blows with the reverse grip can come in a staccato, pecking motion from the elbow rather than full force from the shoulder, rather as you would pick ice, and still cause harm and death. Blade writer James LaFond believes that most reverse grip, icepick-style attacks are delivered that way, at least today.[7] This should not be surprising, really, since it does not take much force to penetrate the body of an unarmored person.

Do not deliver this blow from above the head with the arm extended like a swinging pendulum.

Overhead, Diagonal from the Right

This downward diagonal blow is, according to Fiore's Getty manuscript, good for attacks from the height of the elbows to the head. Fiore discouraged attacks using the reverse grip at targets below the level of the elbows: "from the elbow down I do not have sure freedom without much danger, and of this strike I have doubts." Fiore, however, approves of this blow because of your ability to cover your enemy's blade with your left hand as you strike.

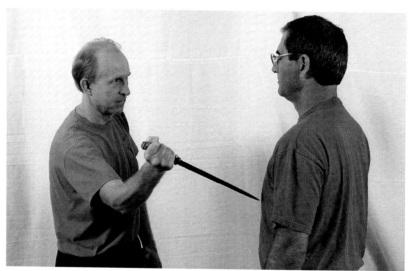

Overhead strike, diagonal from the right.

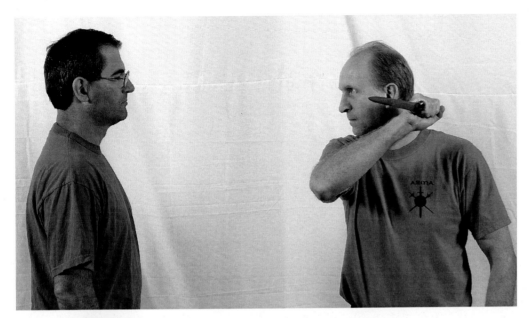

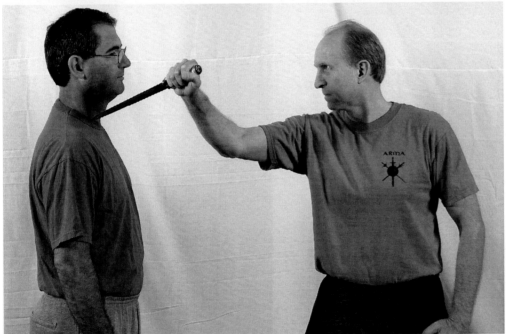

Overhead strike, diagonal from the left.

Overhead, Diagonal from the Left

Expressly described by Fiore and Meyer, this blow starts at the left ear and attacks from the level of the elbow to the head. As before, it is not recommended for attacks below the level of the elbow because it exposes you to attack.

Moreover, Fiore cautioned that "those blows from the left he cannot do being ready to make a cover against his enemy." In other words, you expose yourself to a stop hit if you attack from the left side. If you are left-handed, this advice applies to a blow from your right.

29

A backhand horizontal strike.

Backhand Horizontal

This blow is shown in the *Gladiatoria* and Fiore. It can be directed at any point between the waist and the temple.

A strike from below.

Below

As far as I am aware, the only source to show this blow is the *Codex Wallerstein*. This strike suffers from the same problem as the blow from the left: you cannot cover against your opponent's blade as you strike, and you expose yourself to his counterblow.

Straight thrust with the forward grip.

Forward Grip

There were four blows with the forward grip: straight thrust, thrust above, hooking from the right, and hooking from the left.

Straight Thrust

Often referred to as the "thrust from below," this straight grip attack is most often depicted aimed at the stomach, or as Fiore says, below the chest. When aimed at the stomach, the *Codex Wallerstein* calls it the "Italian thrust." However, this versatile thrust can be directed at any part of the body from the head to the groin, including the hands and arms. It can be delivered in a variety of ways, from a full-power punching style to short, staccato attacks and feints.[8]

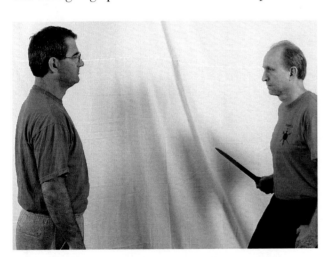

The thrust above with the forward grip.

Thrust Above

The *Codex Wallerstein* calls this blow the "French thrust." It is characterized by the inversion of the hand as the blow travels to the target so that at impact the thumb is down, the fingers are up, and in a right-hander the palm is facing to the right. In sword fencing, this hand position has been called "prime," or first position.

31

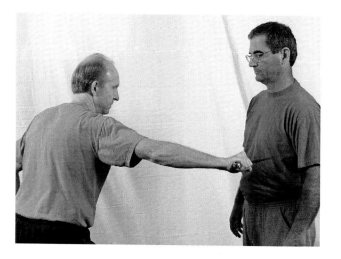

Hooking from the right.

Hooking from the Right

Although no manual of which I am aware expressly shows this blow, it is inferred from the *Gladiatoria*, which depicts a defense against a backhanded blow from the defender's left (attacker's right).

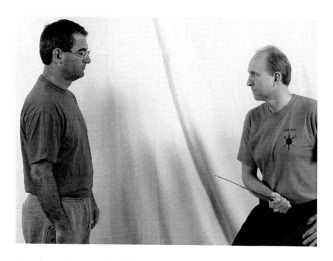

Hooking from the left.

Hooking from the Left

The opposite blow is also inferred.

FOOTWORK

The purpose of footwork is either to bring you within distance to the true place (the location where you can launch a blow without having to take a step) or to avoid a blow either by retreat or a sideways movement. In dagger work, you must always remain in motion. However, despite the importance of motion to dagger play, the manuals generally do not discuss footwork in connection with the techniques. This is especially notable in connection with the unarmed defenses. When practicing the unarmed defenses, many people combine them with sidesteps on the theory that evasions should always be employed. But I think that the old masters purposefully do not generally discuss evasions in conjunction with dagger techniques. In my opinion, the techniques set out in the manuals are designed to work in the worst-case scenario. That worst case is the dagger attack at its most dangerous—when the attack is sudden and launched from such a close distance that the defender will be lucky if he has enough time to get his hands in play to cover the attack. In that situation, the defender generally won't have time to evade as well. Thus, the covers and the techniques that follow must work without an evasion. The dagger defenses, particularly Fiore's unarmed plays, seem to meet this test.

You can, of course, couple your dagger plays with evasions and footwork, and the old masters were not ignorant of the need to do so. Meyer, for instance, in one play advises joining a cover with a turning movement of the body. But that advice is an exception to the otherwise deafening silence about evasive body shifting in the majority of manuals.

Still, we cannot ignore the need to understand basic footwork and body shifting so that we can combine them with our plays when it is possible to do so. Since the old masters viewed their arts as integrated, it is likely that they expected dagger combat to employ the same footwork as swordplay. Don't expect anything surprising, extraordinary, or complicated about this footwork. It is simple, straightforward, and easy to understand and execute.

These steps are shown going forward. Except for the lunge, they can also be done going backward. For instance, the reverse passing step would be simply a step backward. Indeed, the reverse passing step is a major defensive move.

The primary means of stepping, derived with one exception from Meyer's swordplay, are as follows.

 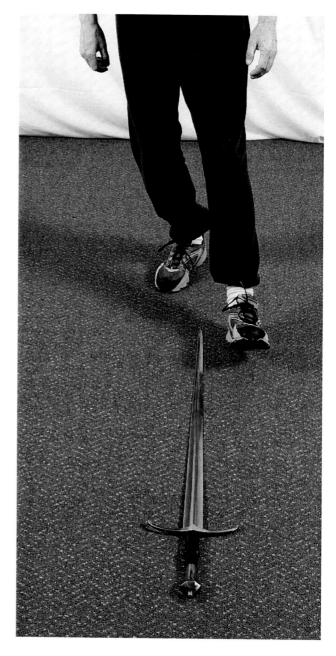

Passing step.

Passing Step

This is just a step forward or backward. Passes forward typically accompany attacks, while passes backward were a major means of defense, since to pass back simply takes your body out of the way of the blow.

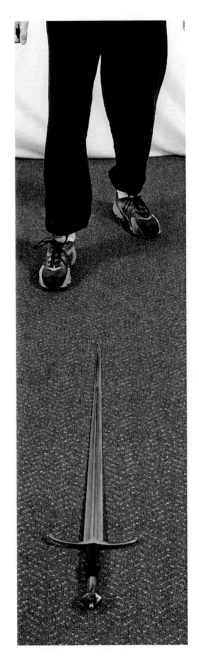  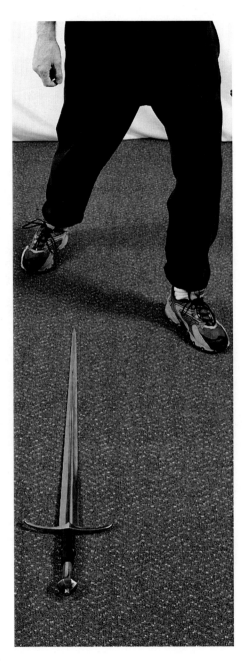

Pass to the diagonal.

Pass to the Diagonal

Passing steps can also be done on the forward and backward diagonals. Depicted here is a forward diagonal pass.

Gathering step.

Gathering Step
To perform the gathering step, first move the lead foot forward, then bring the rear foot up. Like the pass, the gathering step can be done backward. Then, move the rear foot first and follow with the front foot.

Hidden step.

Hidden Step

This is the opposite of the gathering step. Move the rear foot toward the front foot, then move the front foot forward. This may have been called the hidden step because the movement of the rear foot may be harder to detect than an initial move with the front foot, allowing the fighter to "steal" some space on his opponent.

Lunge

Everyone is familiar with the lunge. It is rather like the gathering step in that the forward foot is propelled toward the enemy, but it generally covers greater distance. The rear foot may or may not be brought forward itself, depending on the amount of distance covered.

 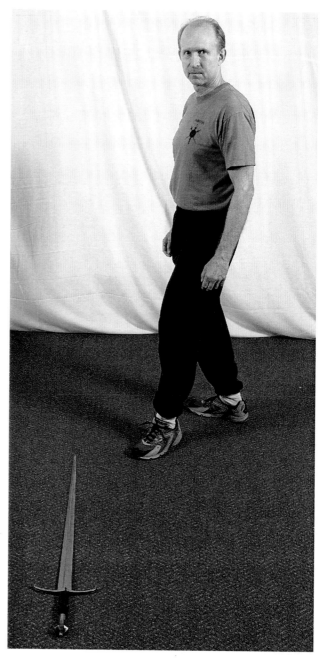

Triangle step.

Triangle Step

This is an off-line movement. It can be done with or without a movement of the front foot. Here, however, we show a triangle step involving movement of the lead foot. To perform this step, move the front foot a short distance to the side or to the front diagonal. Follow with the rear foot but in bringing it forward, move it farther off line. This will displace the body and is often used to avoid blows. It is an extremely useful step to master, but for many students it does not seem to come naturally and requires considerable practice.

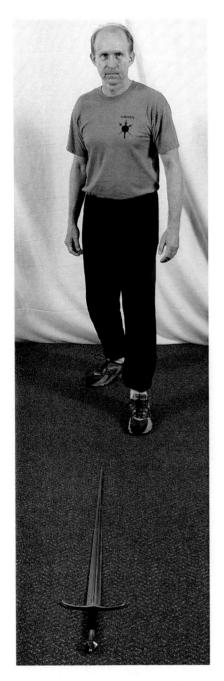  

Pass and triangle step.

Pass and Triangle Step

In this version of the triangle step, the first movement is a passing diagonal step. What becomes the rear foot after the pass is brought behind the lead foot, crossing behind so it takes the body well off line.

 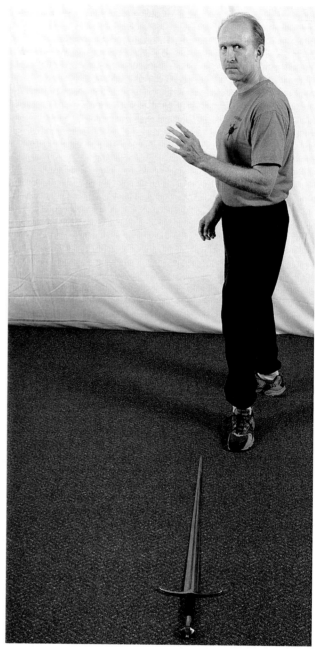

Triangle step.

Turn

This is like the triangle step but involves more of a turn of the body to get it out of the way of a blow than a true triangle step.

Striking a blow "on the pass" (while stepping forward with the rear foot).

Blows and Footwork

If you and your enemy are close enough to touch without moving your feet, there is little need for footwork, but that is not always the case. If the general body positions shown in the manuals' illustrations are any guide, blows originating out of distance appear mainly to have been delivered "on the pass"—that is, the blow was delivered while stepping forward with the rear foot. To make such a blow in true time if you are right-handed, you begin with the right foot back. Move the hand first, follow with the body, then make the step, bringing the right foot in front of the left so at the end of the blow, the right foot is the leading foot.

Some commentators argue that the foot and the hand must end their movement at the same time. George Silver argued against this, and I believe he was correct. If you tie the hand to the movement of the foot, the blow will be slower to land than if you let the foot follow the blow and hit the ground after the blow hits the target. The slower the blow, the greater the enemy's chance to cover it or to deliver a stop hit. I discuss the basis for this opinion in more detail in chapter seven.

Although the sources do not describe attacks delivered by stepping to the diagonal or with any other step, there is no reason why you cannot do so.

COVERING—THE FIRST CRUCIAL STEP

At first and foremost in all dagger fighting is that you diligently address all stabs wherever they come so you can be in the way with the hand and quickly attend to your deeds.
—Andreas Lignitzer

"Covering" means interdicting lines of attack and intercepting, deflecting, and controlling the dagger arm. It is a crucial fundamental concept in armed and unarmed dagger combat. Mastery of covering is essential to survival. This does not mean that evading the attack with footwork, either by retreat or sidestep, is not advisable; rather, the defenses in the manuals appear to assume that you do not have the time or the space to evade, and so you must cover or die.

The first objective of the cover generally is to interdict the line of attack. This does not necessary mean "block," as that concept is used in Asian martial arts. It means placing your hand or forearm in opposition to the trajectory of your enemy's forearm (the delivery system for the dagger) in such a manner that he is unable to bring the weapon to its intended strike point. If

you intercept the arm, you interrupt the attack at worst and stifle it at best. Thus, the cover first acts to deflect the attack away from the body or otherwise bar its progress. The second objective of all covers is to gain control of the attacker's arm. All the unarmed defenses and many armed defenses flow from this initial contact and how it is made.

The emphasis on catching or controlling the enemy's arm springs from three practical considerations. First, most dagger attacks, like most knife attacks today, took place within distance at the "true place"; that is, they normally occurred when the enemy was close enough to touch the victim with his hand without taking a step. Attacks at this range are extremely dangerous because they come so fast that the victim usually has little chance to defend or move out of the way.

Second, a dagger-wielding enemy, like a knifer today, rarely contented himself with a single strike. If the first blow missed, the enemy could be counted on to follow up with continuous afterstrikes until the victim was dead. This is a feature of many knife attacks today—think of how often we read news stories of a knifing victim who suffered 10, 20, even 40 blows. There is no reason to believe that human behavior was any different 600 years ago. Thus, immediate control of the knife arm is essential to prevent the enemy from continuing his attack with multiple strikes and to enable the mounting of an effective defense after the attack is neutralized. Medieval and Renaissance unarmed defenses emphasize such immediate control. The attacker ideally should get just one blow; then he is yours.

Third, the target of the cover should be the attacker's forearm, not his knife hand. Trying to grasp the knife hand too often results in a blade grab, which can incapacitate your hand.[9]

Therefore, the student must pay serious attention to the covers. Survival depends on whether a cover is done effectively.

The cover chosen to meet an attack depends on several factors. First, consider the nature of the attack. Is it a reverse-grip stab or a forward-grip stab? Second, at what angle does it approach your body? Does it come straight in or at an angle or with a hooking motion? Does it approach from above or below? Third, where are your hands when you perceive the attack? Are they to the inside of the attacking arm or the outside? Are they high, at chest level, or are they low, at waist level? Where your hands are at the moment you perceive the attack is important; your cover will move from where your hands are to intercept the attacker's forearm. They should not "re-set" to another position before initiating the cover, a time-wasting habit one often sees in knife defenses advocated by some modern martial arts systems. In a dagger or knife attack, you cannot afford to waste a millisecond.

With these concerns in mind, let's now consider the primary methods of covering.

Covering for Blows from Above

First, there are the covers for blows from above, the common "ice-pick" stab with the reverse grip.

One-Handed Method

The primary defense is to catch the arm using one of your own hands. The manuals do not say how this is done. They only say something like "catch his arm behind the wrist and step behind him and throw him to the ground." Sometimes the technique is illustrated with a drawing, but usually it will show the enemy's arm after it is grasped, as shown in this image from Fiore's Pisani-Dossi manuscript, published in the 19th century by Novati.

We have to infer how to perform the cover and catch. Many people try to catch the arm with the palm of the hand, but in my opinion this is neither safe nor effective. Your wrist is nothing more than a hinge. A powerful blow—and you

An image from Fiore dei Liberi's *Flos Duellatorum* illustrates the one-handed method of covering for blows from above. (Note: All of the *Flos Duellatorum* illustrations used in this book were scanned from the Pisani-Dossi version.)

have to assume that the blow will be powerful—can burst through the hinge of your wrist and strike you in the head or chest. You can bet your life on this method if you like, but I do not recommend it.

I suspect that medieval and Renaissance fighters caught the arm in ways like those practiced by Japanese and Chinese fighters using

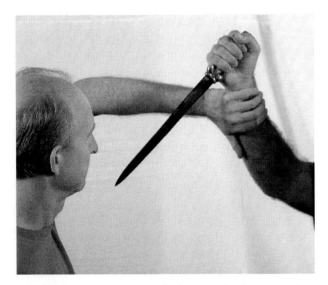

A fighter attempts to catch the attacker's arm with the palm of his hand. This is not the recommended method.

jujutsu and chin-na. That is, they intercepted the arm with the edge of the hand or on the forearm as near to the wrist as circumstances allowed, and then rolled the hand onto the attacker's forearm.

The action is not two separate movements, but one continuous, smooth one: contact and then roll to grasp. The advantage of making initial contact with the edge or outside of the hand or arm is that your forearm acts as a barrier to the downward attack. While blocking in this manner may lead to a wounded arm, this is far preferable to receiving a stab to the body. You can fight on with an injured arm.

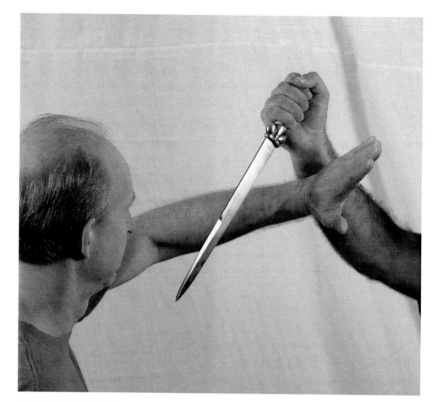

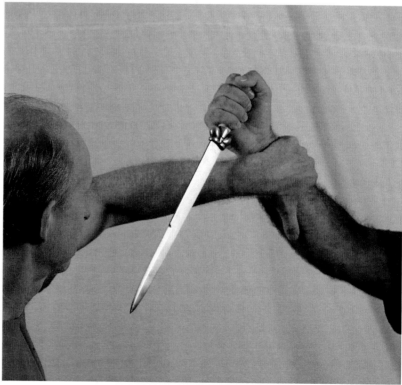

The fighter intercepts with the edge of his hand, then rolls his hand onto his attacker's forearm.

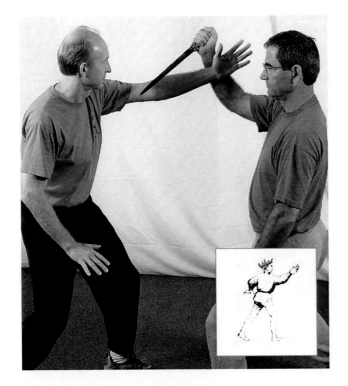

Compare the covering techniques in the photo with Fiore's drawing of *posta longa*, shown in inset.

That medieval and Renaissance fighters' techniques probably mirrored the methods of other martial systems can be inferred from the approach to combat wrestling advocated by Fiore. Fiore describes a *posta*, or posture, called *posta longa* for wrestling.

Fiore specifically says that this *posta* is good for securing grips. *Posta longa* is well suited for intercepting a blow from above with the dagger. This *posta longa* mirrors the drawings in Fiore's books. (Note that the hand is perpendicular to the ground. This is how Fiore's drawings illustrate the *posta*.) I personally prefer positioning the hand with the palm facing either toward the ground or the enemy's face, which feels more natural to me and seems to allow me to obtain the grip a little quicker. But you can catch the arm effectively either way. You must make up your own mind which method you prefer.

The method of initial contact against a blow from above is the same regardless of whether you defend with your left or right hand.

This cover was called the "reverse hand" by Meyer.

Meyer calls this type of cover, where your thumb stands toward the enemy's elbow after the grip, the "reverse hand."

When the enemy is directly in front and your arms are down or to the outside of the attack, you perform a different cover, which sweeps across the path of the attack in a fanning movement.

This cover sweeps across the path of the attack in a fanning movement.

Fiore is critical of this cover, but it is shown or described in a number of manuals, Meyer among them. Meyer calls the resulting grip the "straight grip" or "straight hand." He advocates its use against thrusts as well.

In this two-handed cover, the force of the attack is blocked by the heels of the defender's hands.

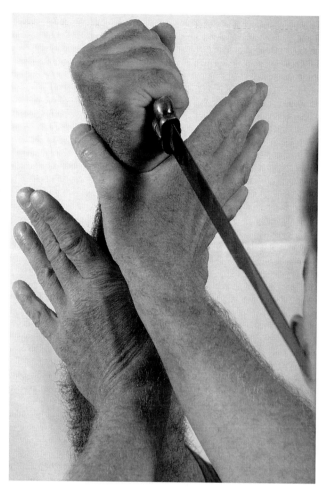

Two-Handed Method

The blow from above can also be met with two hands. There are two methods for doing so.

The first such cover involves what appears to be a simple catch of the arm. Note how the wrists are turned so that the heels are directly beneath the enemy's forearm. If you cover in this manner, the heels will take the force of the blow, and since they are supported directly by your forearms, this enables you to withstand a very hard blow. In an emergency—the classic "Oh, $#!%" moment—you can catch a blow one-handed in this fashion as long as you take the blow on the heel, but it is risky.

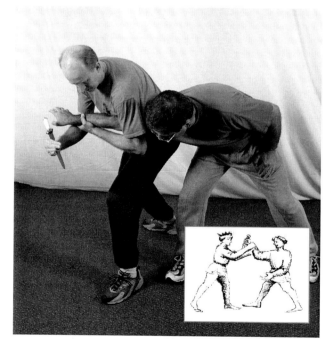

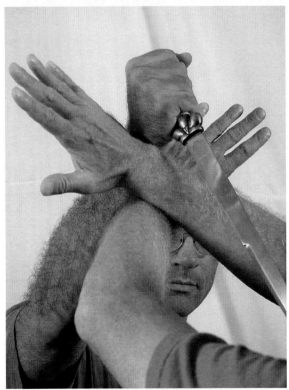

Here, the force is blocked by the defender's crossed arms.

The second two-handed cover uses crossed arms. Some modern knife-fighting experts dismiss this cover as impractical.[10] However, it appears in both Eastern and Western fighting arts.[11] Given that the authors of the Western manuals had practical experience with dagger fighting, they must have found this technique useful.

The cover with crossed hands seems to address a problem inherent in covering with a single arm. When covering with a single arm, there is the chance that the force and speed of the blow will be so great that the enemy's arm will slide off yours before you can obtain a grip. Crossing the arms to cover prevents this slide, because the funnel created by the crossed arms traps the enemy's arm.

Fiore says the crossed-arms cover is best reserved for fighting in armor because the cover does not reach out far from the body. There seems to be some truth in Fiore's statement. The crossed-arms cover generally does not efficiently meet blows as far from the body as a single-arm cover. When the enemy's blade is short, this does not matter so much. But when the blade is up to 12 inches long, as many medieval blades were, you risk getting stabbed in the face when using the crossed-arms cover against a blow from above.

49

The straight thrust.

The straight thrust—the "thrust from below"—is generally aimed at the body from the nipples or below. To perform the primary cover against this blow, roll both hands onto the top of the enemy's forearm and grasp it tightly.

Do not raise your hands up high before making contact. This takes too much time, and in a dagger attack fractions of a second are precious.

Make the smallest roll possible. It is essential that you place the heels of your hands on the *top* of the forearm.

Proving that there is nothing new under the sun, the U.S. Army's unarmed combat manual of the 1950s and the U.S. Marine Corps manual of 1999 illustrate a similar two-handed cover against the thrust from below.

Make sure the heels of your hand are on top of the attacker's forearm when performing the two-hand cover.

Meyer describes striking the enemy's arm away, although he does not picture it. Paulus Kal and the Solothurner manual illustrate striking-away blows in a manner similar to the karate downward knife-hand block.

Striking away is described only in dagger-to-dagger combat, and the cover is immediately followed by a counterblow with the dagger. However, striking away could be used in unarmed defense if you are not in position to do anything else. (What counts is what works, after all.) But it is a weak response if it does not immediately lead to a grip. A method for obtaining a grip after striking away will be illustrated later.

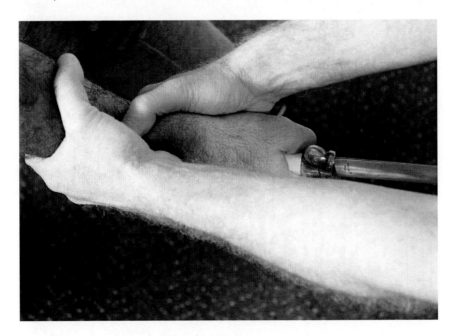

This is the wrong way to perform the cover. If you make contact with your palms on the sides of his forearm and your thumbs on top, the force of his blow can drive through the gates of your thumbs and you will be stabbed.

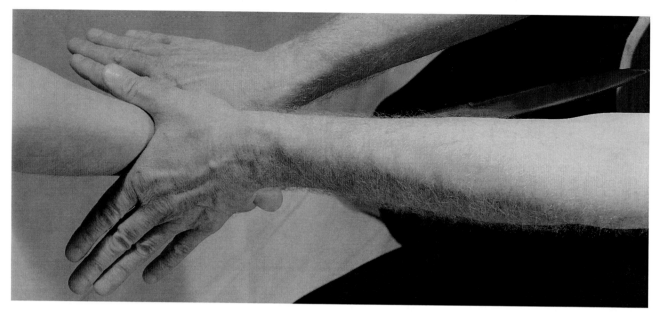

This cover, taught by legendary knife combat instructor Hock Hochheim and shown in his book, *Military Knife Combat,* is also demonstrated in the U.S. Army's *Hand-to-Hand Combat* (FM 21-150) and the U.S. Marine Corps' *Close Combat* (MCRP 3-02B). It is similar to one taught by the medieval and Renaissance masters.

Here is a cover done with one hand, as propounded by Vadi.

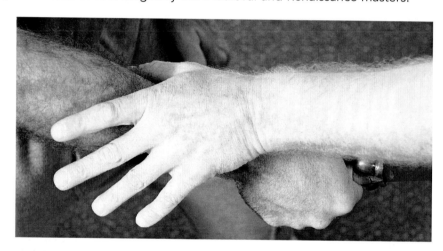

This striking-away blow, which can be found in Paulus Kal's works and in the Solothurner manual, is similar to the downward knife-hand block in karate. Meyer also describes striking away and "parrying strongly."

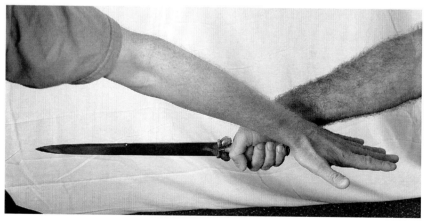

THE ROLE OF WRESTLING

Onward from here as you come forth with your stab pay attention that you also block your opponent's stab with your single hand so that one can come to the work of arm breaking, foot trapping and wrestling.

—Andreas Lignitzer

All the dagger-fighting techniques that follow, including those in dagger-to-dagger combat, are based on wrestling. Meyer declared, "grappling is extremely important with the dagger." Fiore said that wrestling was the foundation of dagger fighting—indeed, of all medieval martial arts, including that of the sword. This is not the kind of wresting we are used to seeing in Olympic or collegiate competition, but an ancient style of wrestling that may go back more than 2,500 years in Europe.[12] The medieval and Renaissance Germans called this method *kampfringen*, or simply, *ringen*.

The techniques are often hard and brutal and can lead to lasting, even permanent, injury. They are not sportive in nature and must be practiced with care if you don't want to injure your training partner.

Anyone familiar with grappling arts understands that you cannot generally go into a bout thinking, "I'm going to do this technique or that technique." The decision to apply one technique in preference to another usually arises in the spur of the moment when the opportunity presents itself. Moreover, the opportunity actually dictates the type of technique you should choose. For instance, if the enemy's arm is bent, apply a technique that relies on the enemy's arm being bent instead of trying to force a straight-armed technique. Conversely, if his arm is straight, attack the arm with one of the techniques that exploits the extended arm. Thus, to apply combat wrestling effectively, you must understand the nature of a given technique, know when it is

most appropriate to apply it, and be able to perceive opportunities as they arise in the flow of battle.

You also need to be flexible. No matter how good you are, sometimes when you try a technique it will fail or it may be countered. You must be able to flow immediately into another technique and, if necessary, a third or even a fourth, until the enemy is defeated. According to Fiore, however, long exchanges consisting of a blow followed by a counter, then a counter to a counter, and a counter to that were the exception rather than the rule. At most, he wrote, the fight went no further than a counter to a counter before a decision was reached.

The Role of Ground Wrestling

There is no doubt that the masters intended you to put your enemy on the ground and finish him there. Depicting an enemy under the feet of the master of the dagger, Fiore said, "They ask me, why I hold this man under my feet, because I have no better place with such a finish with the art of Abrazare."[13]

But few period manuals discuss what to do once you have the enemy on the ground. This has led to major controversy in the modern European martial arts community about the role that ground wrestling played in *kampfringen*. Many people come to the study of historical European martial arts with a sport-oriented, or even a mixed martial arts/grappling background, and they have a hard time believing that ground grappling played no role in medieval and Renaissance combat.

There is no definitive answer yet to the question of how extensive a role it played. However, it is highly likely that ground wrestling played only a limited role in *kampfringen*. Groundwork does not appear to have been aimed at the enemy's submission by the use of chokes or restraints, but was employed to diminish the enemy's capacity for resistance and

Fiore illustrates use of the crossed arms against the straight thrust from below, as recreated in this photo.

This cover uses crossed arms. The *Gladiatoria* alone of the manuals of which I am aware shows how to defend against a hooking thrust from below or one coming from the side rather than straight on.

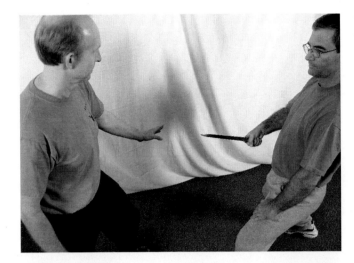

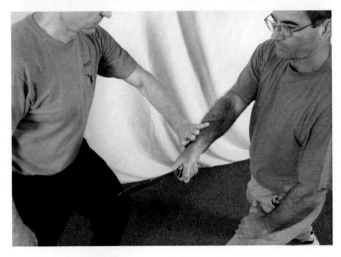

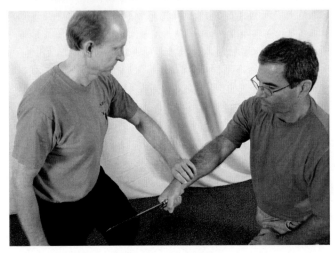

Meyer advocates use of a one-handed cover against a straight thrust from below.

to enable the defender to deploy his own weapon. For example, the *Gladiatoria* is one of the few manuals to illustrate and describe groundwork in any detail for dagger combat. It sets out seven techniques for pinning the enemy. In every instance, pinning is intended to secure the enemy so the defender can use his dagger. While some grappling on the ground is depicted in Talhoffer, ground techniques are not described. And in one telling drawing, one man kneels on the arm of a fallen enemy while holding his arm as he stabs with his dagger.

Practice involving wrestling on the ground with a dagger indicates that this creates a very dangerous situation for the man who does not have the weapon. Even if he locks up his opponent, it is often relatively easy for the enemy to shift the weapon to the other hand and "kill" the defender. One's options on the ground are severely limited. Covers are more difficult to perform because of the speed of the attack. Mobility is lost. Chokes, a mainstay of sportive submission wrestling, are of virtually no use to the defender if the enemy remains in possession of the knife.

It thus appears that the purpose of throwing an enemy to the ground was to break an arm either as he fell or after he lay vulnerable on the ground, or to secure him long enough for the defender to deploy his dagger to finish the engagement.

This conclusion is consistent with the tactics of kumi-uchi, a forerunner of classical jujutsu that focused on battlefield grappling in armor. Throwing and locking were the primary initial methods of kumi-uchi. Ground grappling played only a supporting, and rather minor, role. "Regardless of the tactics used to overcome an enemy the *coup de grace* would usually be given with the heavy-duty dagger known as yoroi doshi . . . Being able to reach one's dagger, or the enemy's for that matter, could mean the difference between life and death in the critical last stage of close combat."[14] Interestingly, the finishing methods on the ground in kumi-uchi and ringen appear to have been very similar: Both often involved stepping or kneeling on one of the enemy's arms or legs to pin him so that decisive blows with the dagger could be administered.[15]

THE USE OF BLOWS

As we have seen, the primary means of unarmed defense against the dagger was based on wrestling. This may be because the techniques were intended for use in armor as well as without, and blows have limited utility against an armored opponent. Certainly, blows can be useful, even in armor. A palm heel blow to the helmet of an armored enemy, like a stiff arm in football, can stun the opponent and render him vulnerable to a follow-up armlock or throw. Anglo points out that there are illustrations showing the German Emperor Maximilian I kicking an armored opponent in the knee during a combat with war hammers, so one must conclude that kicks and blows could also be used in armored dagger fighting.[16] Meyer advocates blows with the dagger pommel in combination with stabs, but by his day—the late 1500s— most men did not fight in full harness. However, unless the hand is encased in a gauntlet, a punch is more likely to harm the defender than the enemy. In any case, the blow was not considered to be decisive. The lock, the throw, and ultimately one's own dagger were expected to end the contest.

Yet, the masters understood that empty-hand blows have their place in dagger combat. Although few manuals describe combining covers and locks with blows, we can see this practice illustrated in at least two of the major sources available to us. In the *Codex Wallerstein* there are several examples of locks combined with blows. The other notable exception is in Talhoffer, 1459. One picture shows the defender covering a dagger blow from above with the

right hand. The defender holds his clenched left hand by his head. The text says, "here he has responded to the thrust and will punch him in the mouth with his fist."[17]

So don't feel that combining covers, wrestling, striking with the empty hand, or kicking is inauthentic even though this is not described in detail in any period manual.

ENDNOTES

1. Oddly, today the U.S. Marine Corps close-combat manual recommends carrying the combat knife on the weak (generally left) side. U.S. Marine Corps. *Close Combat (MCRP 3-02B)*. Washington, DC, 1999, pp. 3-02B.
2. Ibid.
3. Sydney Anglo. *The Martial Arts of Renaissance Europe*. New Haven: Yale University Press, 2000, pp. 178–179.
4. Nicholas Sekunda. *Marathon 490 BC: The First Persian Invasion of Greece*. Oxford, England: Osprey, 2002, p. 8. The dagger depicted on the vase has a round pommel, long quillons, and a fuller, a design that appears in medieval and Renaissance Europe thousands of years later. The dagger appears to be double-edged.
5. Some modern knife systems advocate and practice cuts from the reverse grip. No medieval and Renaissance manual depicts blows of this type. Indeed, in the real world of combat it appears reverse-grip cuts are not used. In his study of knife attacks in Baltimore, LaFond claims that he was unable to document a single instance in which a reverse-grip cut was employed. James LaFond. *The Logic of Steel*. Boulder, CO: Paladin Press, 2001, p. 18.
6. Fiore, Getty MS. Translated by Lovett, Davidson, and Lancaster.
7. LaFond, p. 18.

8. The *Codex Wallerstein* calls this the Italian thrust.

9. LaFond, p. 40. "The most crippling long-term stroke is the cut or stab to the opponent's hand. I know of four stabbing victims who lost the use of their right hand after the tendons were severed attempting to grab a knifer's blade hand."

10. Peyton Quinn. *Defending Against the Blade.* Lake George, CO: Curve Productions, 1990. Quinn dismisses the crossed-arm cover as useless. Hock Hochheim, however, discusses it in his book *Knife Fighting Encyclopedia* (p. 175). Interestingly, Hochheim's photos of the crossed-arm cover look identical to the drawings of the cover in the *Gladiatoria.* However, he does not bring up both arms simultaneously, but one right after the other.

11. *Abwehr Englischer Gangster-Methoden.* Norway: P.K. DES A.O.K., 1942, p. 17. This is a Wehrmacht unarmed combat manual. Its techniques appear to be derived from judo.

12. For instance, techniques like the one the medieval and Renaissance Germans called the "short hip" throw in the mid-1400s were practiced 2,500 years ago by the Greeks. Compare Talhoffer (plate 194) with Stephen Miller's *Ancient Greek Athletics* (p. 49, fig. 76). Judo stylists know this throw as tai-oto-shi; ninpo stylists as ganseki-nage. In its many variations, it is one of the most effective and practical throws in the grappling arsenal of any martial system.

13. Fiore (Getty MS).

14. Serge Mol. *Classical Fighting Arts of Japan: A Complete Guide to Koryu Jujutsu.* New York: Kodansha International, 2001, p. 31.

15. Compare Mol (p. 32) and Christian Henry Tobler's *Secrets of German Medieval Swordsmanship: Sigmund Ringeck's Commentaries on Master Liechtenauer's Verse* (pp. 223–228).

16. Anglo, plate XIV.

17. Hans Talhoffer (1459), Brian Hunt translator, unpublished manuscript.

CHAPTER 5

UNARMED AGAINST THE DAGGER

If he has drawn his dagger but you have not and he stabs above at you . . .

—Andreas Lignitzer

Unarmed defense against a short-edged weapon such as the dagger is one of the greatest challenges in personal self-defense. W.E. Fairbairn, Shanghai policeman, celebrated martial artist of the mid-20th century, and trainer of World War II British commandos, once wrote, "it is admitted by recognized authorities that for an entirely unarmed man there is no certain defence against a knife."[1] The ancient masters understood this, too. Bob Charron, an expert on the methods of Fiore dei Liberi, says that Fiore regarded the dagger as the most dangerous weapon of all because of its speed and the difficulty in defending against it.[2] Echoing that concern, Talhoffer wrote in his 1467 treatise at the start of the dagger section, "Now we take up the dagger. God preserve us all!"[3] He expressed no similar sentiment about any other weapon.

Since virtually every medieval and Renaissance man carried a knife or dagger, the possibility of a dagger attack was ever-present. The London coroner's rolls for 1300–1378 describe many such assaults, but few deaths from dagger-to-dagger combat. In these assaults the victim usually was unarmed in the sense that he may have had a dagger or knife himself, but he did not have time to deploy it to meet the attack.[4] That the old masters understood this dynamic is clearly illustrated in the *Gladiatoria*, where the anonymous author often prefaces empty-hand defenses like this: "The third technique of the dagger: if he thrusts at your body from below, and you cannot get to your dagger . . ." Hard reality forced medieval and Renaissance men to devise efficient means of defeating a dagger attack while unarmed.

These techniques are as useful and effective today as they were 600 years ago.[5]

THE GUARDS

Modern knife attacks are usually so spontaneous and quick that the victim rarely has the chance to fall into a formal guard, a position of readiness from which to attack or defend. The London coroners' rolls indicate that things were no different in the past. Thus, it is not surprising that most manuals do not describe specific unarmed guards against the dagger. Talhoffer's 1467 manual describes an unarmed guard, but the posture is of an unarmed man facing a sword attack. However, given that the old masters viewed their art as integrated, one can infer that Talhoffer would use such a posture against the dagger. Practically alone of the medieval and Renaissance manuscripts, Fiore's Getty work illustrates several unarmed guards that seem

specifically intended to face the dagger. A sample follows.

Probably the best of the guards is Fiore's guard for general wrestling called the "full iron door." I find this to be a most useful ready position. You are well balanced and able to move in all directions, and your hands are positioned in such a way that they can respond to an attack at high and low levels.

Fiore's "full iron door doubled" requires the defender to ready himself with his arms crossed in front at the wrists, which he holds at waist level. The Getty manuscript says that this guard is best used with fighting armor because your covers are too close to the body for real safety.

The full iron door position.

The full iron door doubled position.

SECTION I: DEFENSES AGAINST THE THRUST FROM ABOVE

Defenses against the thrust from above, or the reverse grip ice-pick style attack, far outnumber those described for the straight thrust in the forward grip. Thus, while the old masters knew and prepared for the straight thrust, they seem far more concerned about the thrust from above and devoted far more time training to defeat it, if the space given to it in the manuals is any indication.

The reason for this may be that the medieval and Renaissance dagger probably was used, more often than not, in the reverse grip. In his book on the evolution of the dagger and fighting knife, Harold Peterson claims he reviewed all contemporary European art he could find containing scenes involving dagger combat. The vast majority showed the thrust from above in the reverse grip.[6] Peterson also argues that the European dagger, such as the rondel with its often-large pommel disk, was designed largely for use with the thrust from above.[7] The thrust from above is the most powerful blow that can be delivered with the reverse grip. It is also a very natural blow. Men untrained in the knife or dagger use it without thinking.[8] How often a knife attacker today will resort to the overhand/thrust from above is

hard to document. James LaFond claims that about 14 percent of knife attacks today involve the thrust from above in the reverse grip.[9] Capt. R.A. Eades, a Florida Department of Corrections defensive tactics instructor, says that most inmate assaults involving shanks rely on the thrust from above in the hammer or reverse grip.

The medieval and Renaissance preference for the reverse grip may stem from its manner of carry, on the right hip. The weapon can be quickly drawn and deployed in the reverse grip from this carry.

We do not picture specific defenses from the cover with crossed hands. The reason is that specific defenses flowing from this cover will be the same as those following a cover with a single left or right hand, depending on how you grip or sweep away the enemy's arm.

The key to performing the crossed-hands cover is not to do it as a static block. It is best performed as in a meet-and-sweep movement, which is fluid rather than static. You can sweep either to the left or the right. Once you decide which direction to go, an opportunity for a defense from a cover by the left or right hand will present itself.

DEFENSES OF THE LEFT HAND

Here are representative defenses against the thrust from above, which begin with a cover by the left hand. We assume that the enemy attacks with the weapon in his right hand.

Twist of the Wrist to Disarm
Source: Fiore

1. Gray (right) attacks with the thrust from above. Black covers with his left hand on the inside of Gray's arm.

2. Black twists Gray's arm downward and counterclockwise.

3. Black then reaches under Gray's arm with his right hand, grasps the blade on the flat and rotates it away from Gray's hand at a 90-degree angle to Gray's forearm.

Black should manipulate the blade so that the dagger's handle rotates through the gap between Gray's fingers and his palm. Dagger-taking is an important skill. Its principles should be well understood and mastered so that live blades can be quickly and safely taken.

Middle Key
Source: Fiore

When the enemy attacks, sometimes the defender is able to cover but fails to obtain a grip on the arm. This is a technique to address that problem.

1. Gray attacks and Black covers but misses his grip and immediately slides his arm over and around under Gray's.

2. While securing the over bind, Black turns his body so that he and Gray end up facing in the same direction. This gives Black the lock called the middle key. Black's hand ideally should be on Gray's elbow, or as close as he can get it.

3. Black uses the middle key to take Gray to the ground.

To bring Gray down, Black levers upward on Gray's trapped elbow. Black can reinforce his leverage on Gray's arm by clasping his hands (not shown).

Fiore referred to the lock as a "key" lock because the bent arm is twisted like a key in a lock. There are upper keys, with the arm high, middle, and lower keys. The lower key is called the "chicken wing" in some grappling systems, such as shootfighting.

Sometimes this technique will fail in that Gray's arm will not bend but instead will remain straight. This is not a cause for concern if Black maintains his over bind. If the technique fails in this way, Black simply strikes Gray on the chin with a palm heel, steps behind Gray's right leg with his right leg, and throws Gray to the ground.

First Upper Key, the Elbow Cup
Source: Fiore

1. Gray attacks and Black covers, obtaining his grip.

2. Black pushes Gray's arm up and back. At the same time, Black cups Gray's elbow with his right hand and steps as deeply as possible behind Gray with his right leg.

3. Black levers the arm by pressing Gray's hand down and his elbow up. The movement should feel rotational, like turning a wheel. This puts pressure on Gray's shoulder and elbow and forces him to fall.

Second Upper Key, One Hand Inside, One Hand Outside
Source: Fiore

1. Gray attacks. Black covers with his left hand.

2. Black pushes Gray's forearm backward to ensure that his elbow remains bent.

3. Black then snakes his right arm over Gray's left elbow and grasps his own forearm near the wrist. If Gray's arm needs to be bent more to achieve the lock, Black strikes the inside of Gray's elbow with his right hand while pushing forcefully rearward with his left hand before securing his grip on his own arm.

4. Black completes the technique by pressing down on Gray's elbow with his right arm while pushing Gray's left hand to the rear and downward. Black also steps behind Gray with his right foot.

Take care when defending against a long blade that you are not stabbed in the face when attempting this technique.

Over-the-Shoulder Break
Sources: Fiore, Meyer, Vadi

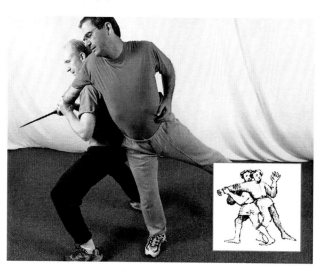

1. When Gray attacks, Black covers but is unable to obtain a grip and Gray's right arm slides off Black's forearm.

2. Black, however, maintains contact with Gray's arm and follows it down, rather like in the wing-chun sticky-hands exercise. When Gray's hand is at the bottom of its trajectory and can go no farther, Black manages to grasp it.

3. Black immediate gives Gray's arm a sharp jerk to pull him off balance, pivots counterclockwise, and raises Gray's elbow to his shoulder. Some people perform this technique by turning in place; however, I think it works better if you pivot so that Black and Gray are back-to-back. It seems to be harder for Gray to counter.

4. When Black has Gray's arm locked, he pulls down sharply to break (or hyperextend) the elbow.

This is one of those techniques that appears intended to deal with the problem of what to do if you cannot immediately obtain a grip after the cover.

Once the grip is obtained, four points are essential. First, you must remember to jerk the arm toward you and downward to break Gray's balance. When Gray is off balance from the jerk, it is harder for him to counter while you pivot. Second, pivot quickly and without hesitation. Any slowness getting Gray's arm to your shoulder allows him to escape. Third, once Gray's arm is over your shoulder, you have no choice but to break it. If you stand in this lock without breaking the elbow, Gray can escape. Fourth, keep the back fairly straight with a slight forward lean. Leaning too far forward makes it hard to lock the arm, and not leaning far enough gives Gray the opportunity to pull Black backward.

This lock can also be followed with a throw, which is not shown here. There are two methods for accomplishing a throw. In the first, Black will bend his knees, keeping his back fairly straight but leaning slightly forward. At the same time he pulls Gray's arm sharply to seat Gray's armpit on the top of his shoulder. Black completes the throw by straightening his legs and bending forward at the waist. Gray will flow over Black's body to the ground, normally landing on his stomach.

In the second, rather than seating Gray's armpit on Black's shoulder, Black grasps Gray's upper right arm or elbow with his left hand and levers Gray over his hip or extended left leg. (Source: Lignitzer)

Taking the Dagger
Source: Fiore

1. When Gray attacks, Black has no room to move to perform an armlock or throw. So the only defense available to him is a dagger-taking. First, Black covers.

2. To take the dagger, Black puts the palm or heel of his hand on the top of the dagger blade.

3. Rotate the dagger blade toward the enemy's elbow on the same plane as the forearm.

It is important to make sure that the dagger blade stays on the plane of the forearm. When it does, the grip will slide out of the gap between the enemy's palm and his little finger.

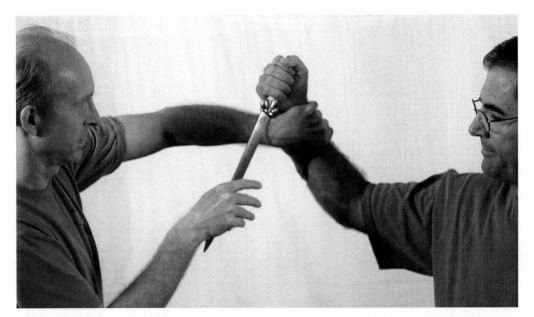

Once the dagger is taken, Black can use it against Gray. Some people make a return stab while the dagger is still in their right hand—while their own hand is on the blade. This runs the risk of the hand sliding along the edge, which can result in injury. Because of this risk, I personally prefer to transfer the weapon to my left hand before countering.

Third Upper Key, Two Hands Outside
Sources: Fiore, Meyer

1. When Gray attacks, Black covers with his left hand. He intercepts the arm while the elbow is still bent. He presses Gray's arm away from him to ensure the elbow stays bent.

2. Black then brings his right arm beneath Gray's attacking arm and grasps Gray so that his hands are close together at Gray's wrist. This puts both of Black's arms to the outside of Gray's arm. At the same time as he reaches with his right hand, Black steps deeply with his right foot to Gray's rear. This unbalances Gray and makes it harder for him to counter.

3. Black then levers Gray to the ground and disarms him for the finish.

Gray's right arm must be intercepted and not allowed to straighten. This technique exploits the bend in the arm. If Gray's arm is not bent enough to acquire the lock, Black can strike the outer part of Gray's elbow with the upper part of his right wrist while pressing forward with his left hand. This will cause the arm to bend. Also, it is preferable for Gray's right foot to be in the lead. If his left foot is in the lead, it will be harder to perform this technique, although it can be done.

A forceful wrench downward after the two-handed grip is obtained can destroy the integrity of Gray's shoulder and elbow, so care should be taken with this technique, as with other locking techniques, so as not to injure the training partner.

Backward Over-the-Leg Throw, Facing Away
Sources: Fiore, Meyer, Marozzo, Vadi, *Gladiatoria*

1. After Black makes his cover, he grasps Gray's throat with his right hand. When he has that grip, he pushes Gray backward to unbalance him, simultaneously stepping behind Gray's extended right leg. Black's hip should touch Gray's hip, and the back of Black's thigh should touch Gray's thigh.

2. At this point, Gray is well off balance. Black completes the throw by pressing Gray downward toward Black's left foot.

This throw, like all wrestling techniques, should be performed in a smooth, continuous motion. There should be no pause between phases. While force is necessary to unbalance Gray, smoothness and suppleness will produce better results than sheer forcefulness, which can be jerky. A palm heel strike to the chin or encircling the neck with the right arm can be substituted for the attack to the throat.

This is a ubiquitous throw and is found in

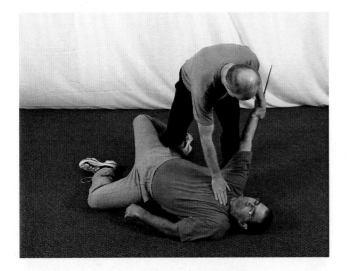

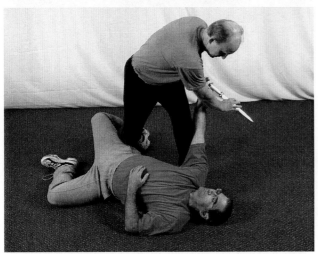

(Left) A cross hook throw is illustrated in *FM 21-150, Unarmed Defense for the American Soldier*, published in 1942 by the U.S. War Department.

many sources. It must have been widely taught and used throughout Europe, and it is a tragedy that it was forgotten. I can tell you from personal experience of having used this throw successfully countless times in armed and unarmed bouts that it is extremely effective, even against larger opponents. If you learn only one wrestling throw, learn this one.

The 16th-century German wrestler Fabian von Auerswald shows a modified version of this throw in which Black's right leg hooks Gray's right exactly like judo's osoto-gari. His is the only period treatise I am aware of, however, to show this cross-hook variation.

Single Left-Hand Cover, Armpit Trap
Sources: Meyer, Fiore, Vadi, *Gladiatoria*

1. As Gray attacks, Black covers with his left hand, which approaches Gray's arm from Gray's outside, using a fanning motion. When Black's hand makes contact with Gray's arm, he grasps using Meyer's "straight grip."

2. Once Black has gripped Gray's hand, he has many options to counter. He could turn and tuck Gray's arm so Gray's elbow is under Black's armpit, for an elbow lock, or he could disarm Gray by grasping the dagger's blade and rotating the point toward Gray's elbow, as described before.

This cover is a natural, instinctive reaction to a sudden, unexpected attack at close range, especially when the enemy is standing directly in front of you and your hands are down and outside the line of attack. The lock is fast, effective, and useful in many situations. You will see this response in connection with other covers and in dagger-to-dagger combat.

As far as I am aware, alone of the masters whose works have been translated into English, Meyer combines the cover with footwork and body shifting in this technique. He says to perform the cover while rotating the body clockwise to get it out of the way of the blow.

Single-Hand Cover and Stab
Sources: Meyer, Fiore extrapolation

1. Black intercepts Gray's stab from above with his left hand.

2. Black fans Gray's forearm to the right, turning his body as necessary to avoid the blow.

3. Black grasps Gray's hand and, using Gray's downward momentum, drives Gray's dagger into his leg or groin.

DEFENSES OF THE RIGHT HAND

Here are some defenses against the blows from above that begin from the cover with the right hand.

Armpit Trap and Disarm
Source: Fiore

1. As Gray attacks, Black covers.

2. If Black obtains a grip, he immediately pivots clockwise and tucks Gray's arm beneath his left arm so that Gray's elbow is in Black's armpit.

3. Black shifts his grip as he tucks Gray's arm so that Black's left hand is now on the arm and his right hand is free. Black then puts pressure on Gray's elbow by lifting up with the left hand and pressing down with the left shoulder on Gray's elbow. It is critical to maintain pressure on Gray's elbow; otherwise, he will escape.

4. Black disarms Gray while Gray is distracted by the pain that should flow from the lock. The disarm is performed by placing the hand on the flat of the blade, using the edge of the palm of the hand. The blade is then rotated out of the palm through the gap between Gray's little finger and his palm.

There are four key points to keep in mind with this technique:

1. Black's left leg must finish the pivot so that it is in front of Gray's right leg. If it does not end there, Gray can escape.

2. When performing the disarm, Black's left hand must pull Gray's hand firmly toward his chest while Black's right hand rotates the dagger blade in the opposite direction. Without this leverage, the dagger will not come free.

3. Ensure that Gray's little finger is up. This will enable maximum pressure on the elbow.

4. The disarm must be performed as soon as Gray's elbow is seated in the armpit. If there is any hesitation, Gray may escape.

The lock can be seated against the chest or stomach. Or Black can drive Gray to the ground, as above, before executing the disarm.

Over-the-Leg Throw, Facing the Same Direction
Sources: Fiore, Meyer, Vadi

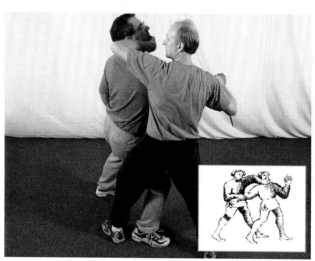 

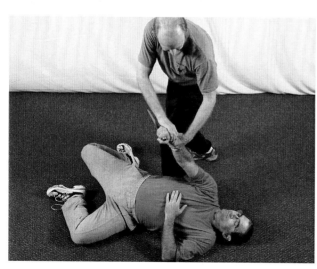 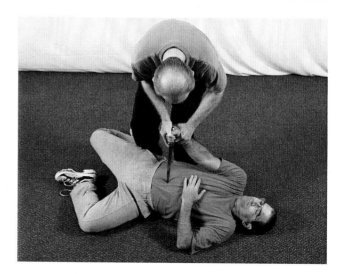

1. Here again, Black's cover fails initially to secure a grip and he retains contact as the attack falls toward the ground.

2. At the bottom of the arc, however, Black manages to secure Gray's arm. Again, seeing Gray's right foot advance, Black steps behind Gray with his *left* foot so that the front of Black's thigh touches the rear of Gray's thigh, blocking movement of Gray's leg.

3. Black reaches up with his left hand, cups Gray's chin from behind, and pulls him backward to the ground.

The grip with Black's left hand does not have to be at the chin, which is the variation advocated by Fiore. It could be anywhere on Gray's upper body. The key principle is to apply backward pressure to Gray's upper body while blocking his right leg with Black's left. Thus, Black could grasp Gray's left shoulder, his collar, around the left side of his head to the chin (shown in Talhoffer 1467), or his hair and still bring him down. Grab what's available quickest. It doesn't have to be pretty, just effective.

One thing to keep in mind is that when Gray falls, he will land *behind* Black, so that Black must be prepared to turn to finish him on the ground.

This is another ubiquitous throw shown in manual after manual in both armed and unarmed combat. It is another highly effective, must-learn throw that can be applied in countless situations. The opportunity for it arises whenever Gray advances a leg toward you. You have only to advance your leg (it doesn't matter if it is your lead leg or you pass forward) behind his to initiate the throw. It is also a counter to the rear bear hug and the hip throw. You are not a complete wrestler without mastery of this technique.

Over-the-Leg Throw, Facing Away
Source: Fiore

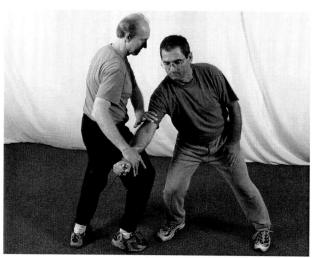
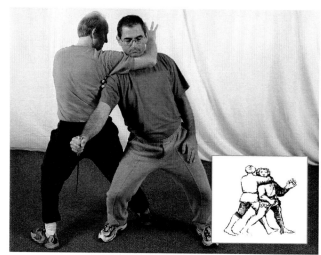

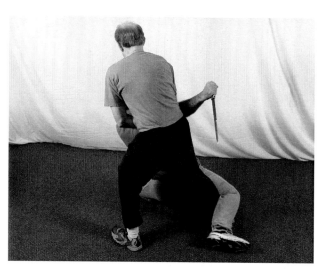

1. When Gray attacks, Black's cover fails to secure a grip on Gray's hand. Because he lacks a secure grip, Black keeps contact with Gray's arm so he retains at least some control of it, until it reaches the end of its trajectory.

2. When Gray's hand reaches the bottom of its arc, Black sees that Gray has advanced his right foot. This presents the opportunity to apply the first over-the-leg throw. Black puts his right leg behind Gray's right leg so their hips and legs are touching. At the same time, Black's right arm encircles Gray's neck. Black and Gray will be facing in opposite directions. At this point, Gray should be off balance and bending backward.

3. Black completes the throw by attempting to touch his left foot with his right hand.

This is another solution to the problem of what to do if Black fails to obtain a grip after the cover. It is a variation of the over-the-leg throw shown earlier. In this version, Black encircles the neck. This is the method advocated by Fiore in this particular situation and is a quick, efficient way to bring a man down.

When entering to encircle the neck, Black must bend forward slightly at the waist. If he enters with his back straight, there is a chance that Gray can unbalance him and throw him with the same technique.

Pressing Arm (or the Straight Arm Bar)
Source: Fiore

1. Black covers the attack and secures a good grip.

2. Black immediately pivots clockwise, pulling on Gray's arm as he turns. At the same time, Black brings his left hand to Gray's elbow to assist the turn and to straighten Gray's arm if it has not already gone straight.

3. At the end of the pivot, Black's left leg should be in front of Gray's right leg. If the pivot

does not end as shown here, it is wrong and Gray can easily escape from the lock.

4. As Black pivots he begins to put pressure on Gray's elbow by pulling up with his right hand and pushing down on Gray's elbow with his left hand. Here Black has completed the pivot and so now applies maximum pressure to the elbow joint. Black should think of trying to drive Gray's right shoulder and face into the ground.

There is no pause between cover, grip, and pivot. These phases of the defense should be one smooth, continuous motion. They do not require strength or sharpness of movement. They require suppleness and speed instead. DO NOT pause so that Gray's body is parallel to the ground and attempt to hold him off the ground in the arm-lock. He will escape. Cover, grip, turn, and drive Gray down all in one motion. Make him kiss the ground, as Fiore said of another technique.

To lock Gray's arm most effectively, make sure his little finger is skyward, straight up, and his palm is perpendicular to the ground. If it is not, his arm can bend, which he can exploit to escape if you are not quick enough with another technique.

There is an alternative to levering Gray's arm and throwing him down. Instead, strike his elbow when it is straight with the forearm or hammerfist. This will break the joint.

Lower Key
Source: Fiore

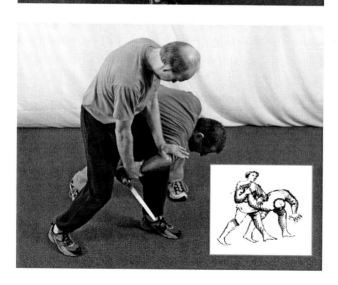

1. Black covers and grips Gray so that Gray's arm remains bent and the force of his blow is spent, such that Gray cannot straighten his arm without effort.

2. Black exploits the opportunity presented by Gray's bent arm. Maintaining his grip on Gray's wrist, Black places his left hand on Gray's elbow.

3. Black applies rotational pressure on the key formed by Gray's bent arm: Black's right hand is pulled toward his body and his left hand pushes away, like turning a crank.

4. Black has options in his footwork, but here he chooses to step forward and to the right, forcing Gray to the ground.

Although not shown, the objective of this lock, like the pressing arm, is to drive Gray to the ground face down.

It is also an alternative to the pressing arm. If Black attempts the pressing arm and Gray succeeds in bending his elbow in an effort to defeat the lock, Black has only to apply this simple bent arm key lock.

Under Bind and Lower Key
Sources: Fiore, *Codex Wallerstein*

This move was also employed in *FM 21-150, Unarmed Defense for the American Soldier* (1942).

1. When Black covers, he misses his grip and, as before, follows Gray's arm down, maintaining contact.

2. When Gray's arm has reach the end of its arc, Black inserts his *left* hand between Gray's arm and his body.

3. Black then snakes his left arm through, under, and around Gray's arm to obtain the *under bind*. Black places his left hand on Gray's elbow, or as near to it as he can get, and presses down. Black's forearm and elbow should cradle Gray's upper arm, and Gray's arm should be bent at a 90-degree angle. As Black presses down with his hand, he presses up with his upper arm so Gray's arm is cranked like a key in a lock. At the same time, Black pivots his body clockwise so that he and Gray end up facing in the same direction.

4. Black ends the technique with a blow to the neck.

While most people associate the edge-of-the-hand blow with Asian martial arts, this blow was known to medieval and Renaissance men. The *Codex Wallerstein* shows it as a finish to this lower key bind.

If Gray's trapped arm does not bend, as sometimes happens, Black should brace Gray's forearm on his upper arm and apply pressure to the elbow. Gray's arm will be locked straight in this position.

DEFENSES OF TWO HANDS

Here are defenses that follow from the cover with two hands.

Armpit Trap
Source: Fiore

1. When Black covers and grips, he immediately turns clockwise, bringing his left arm over the top of Gray's right so that he traps Gray's elbow beneath the left arm in his armpit.

2. Black throws out his left leg and sits forcefully, driving Gray to the ground so he lands on his face.

3. Once Gray is on the ground, Black levers his arm to break it.

An armpit lock is shown in 1942's *FM 21-150, Unarmed Defense for the American Soldier.* The manual does not mention the ground finish.

You have already seen this lock performed from a different cover. I don't mean to be repetitive, but it is important to understand that the techniques can be done from almost any cover. The fact that a technique is shown in connection with one cover doesn't mean it can't be performed from another.

If you understand the principle involved here, you'll see how laughable a stock Hollywood dagger/knife fighting scenario is. In just about every movie involving a knife fight, the hero finds himself in a clinch with the bad guy. Each of them holds the knife arm of the other. They strain and grimace and struggle. How stupid. All the hero has to do is turn, as above, and trap the bad guy's elbow in his armpit.

This lock is common to many martial arts, including chin-na and judo/jujutsu, and was once taught to American soldiers.

First Upper Key, One Hand Inside, One Hand Outside
Source: Fiore

1. After Black obtains his grip, he pushes Gray's arm upward and back to keep the elbow bent.

2. Black exploits the bend by shifting his left hand around the outside of Gray's arm and grabs his own wrist.

3. Black then levers Gray's hand toward the ground, stepping behind Gray with his right foot.

If Gray's arm is not sufficiently bent to apply this lock, a blow with Black's left hand on the crook of Gray's elbow coupled with a simultaneous push backward of Gray's right hand will bend his arm.

This is a very effective technique. The *Codex Wallerstein* shows it as a defense against a right punch.

Second Upper Key, Two Hands Outside
Source: Fiore

1. After Black obtains his grip, he pushes Gray's arm upward and back to keep the elbow bent.

2. Black exploits the bend by snaking his right hand under and around Gray's arm to grip Gray's forearm near the wrist. Gray's elbow rests on Black's shoulder or upper arm.

3. Black levers down with his hands and up with his upper arm to crank the key, and Gray falls.

95

SECTION II: DEFENSES AGAINST THE THRUST FROM BELOW

Although the thrust from above may have been the most likely dagger attack in medieval and Renaissance times, the thrust from below, or straight thrust from the forward grip, probably is the most prevalent type of knife attack today.[10]

Although less common, evidently, in the medieval and Renaissance period, it was still used, for there are numerous defenses to this type of attack found in the *fechtbucher.*

The attack often would be done on the pass, but it is also often pictured without the pass in a motion that must have been much like a karate reverse punch.[11] Reliance on the passing step implies that the attack began at some distance. Depiction of the attack without the pass implies an attack at close range.

DEFENSES FROM THE TWO-HANDED COVER

Grip and Strip
Source: Fiore

1. When Gray attacks, Black covers with two hands. The attack comes so quickly that he can do no more than hike his body backward and away from the blow.

2. Maintaining a grip with the left hand on Gray's arm, Black grasps the blade with the right. Black then takes the dagger by rotating the point toward Gray's elbow. To take the dagger Black must pull with the left hand and push the blade with the right. Care must be taken to rotate the blade along the plane of Gray's forearm. If such care is not taken, the dagger will not come free easily.

3. Black then has his choice of finishes. He can punch, strike, or kick Gray, or even run away.

This is a technique that you may want to employ when you are surrounded by obstacles and have no room to move.

Over-the-Shoulder Break
Source: Fiore

1. Gray attacks and Black covers.

2. When Black has obtained his grip, he jerks sharply on Gray's arm. The jerk should be back and down to pull Gray off balance.

3. When Gray is off balance, Black pivots clockwise toward his right, ending up in a back-to-back position, while raising Gray's arm to his shoulder.

4. When Gray's elbow is seated on Black's shoulder, Black pulls down sharply to break the elbow.

As mentioned earlier, this is not a restraint. If Black attempts to use this lock as a restraint, Gray will eventually escape. The elbow must be broken.

This technique doesn't work as well when the enemy is shorter or substantially taller than the defender.

At an ARMA seminar, a former U.S. Army ranger told me he learned this same technique in the army during the 1960s. It is described in the U.S. Army's *FM 21-150, Hand-to-Hand Combat* (Washington, DC, 1954); however, no similar technique is illustrated in the army's current manual for close combat.

Arm Drag from the Outside
Source: Fiore

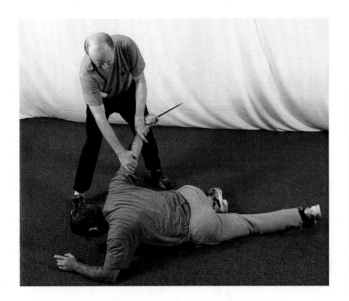 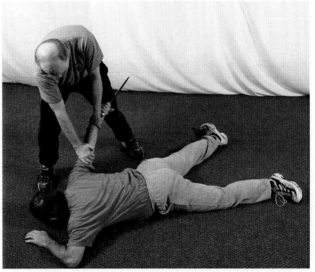

1. Gray attacks and Black covers.

2. Black maintains his grip on Gray's arm with Black's left hand. With his right hand, Black reaches across Gray's arm and grips Gray's elbow on the outside.

3. Black then levers Gray's arm by pushing with his left hand and pulling with his right. This forces Gray's head and shoulders down.

Ultimately, this pressure drives Gray to the floor, where he can be locked up or subdued with blows to the back of the head.

Here, Gray's arm did not bend as he went to ground. Often Gray's arm will bend. In that case, apply a lower key lock rather than the reverse arm bar pictured here.

Arm Strike from the Inside
Source: Fiore

1. Black covers with both hands, as before. Maintaining his grip on Gray's arm with his left hand, this time Black attacks Gray's elbow from the inside line.

2. Black strikes Gray's elbow with the heel of his hand to break the arm.

Instead of a blow to the elbow, Black can execute the technique as an inside arm drag, which will normally result in a lower key lock with Gray face down on the ground. The arm drag is performed essentially in the same manner as the outside arm drag, by pushing with the left hand and pulling with the right to force Gray to fall.

Crossed Arms against the Hooking Thrust
Source: Extrapolation from *Gladiatoria*

1. Gray hooks his thrust from below rather than coming straight in.

2. Black covers with crossed arms.

3. Black then secures Gray's arm in the lower key, snaking underneath to obtain an under bind, while pivoting to face the same direction.

Finish either by driving Gray's face into the ground or striking the back of the neck.

SECTION III: DEFENSES AGAINST THE STRAIGHT THRUST WITH THE ONE-HANDED COVER

Short Hip or Forward Over-the-Leg Throw
Source: Meyer

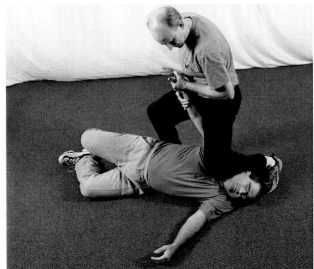

1. Gray thrusts at Black's throat in the forward grip. Black covers with his left hand.

2. His grasp secure, Black steps forward with his right foot and simultaneously reaches beneath Gray's upper arm with his right so that Gray's arm is caught in the crook of his elbow, like a nut in a nutcracker.

3. Black pivots to his left more than 180 degrees. As he completes the pivot, he thrusts his left leg in front of Gray's right, blocking Gray's forward movement.

4. Black completes the throw by continuing to twist his body to the left. This pulls Gray across Black's right leg so that he falls at Black's feet.

The throw goes by various names. In judo it is called tai-otoshi, and Auerswald called it the "short hip."[12] The fact that both Meyer and Auerswald describe it suggests it was well known at the time.

It can also be done against a blow from above.

The pivot should done so that its arc travels through more than 180 degrees.

Done properly, the technique will exploit Gray's forward momentum and will feel almost effortless, requiring virtually no strength. Small men can easily throw large men with this technique. It is an extremely effective throw, and its variations make it adaptable to many situations.

Striking Away
Sources: Talhoffer (1443), Fiore, extrapolation from Meyer,
and *Codex Wallerstein* for the blow

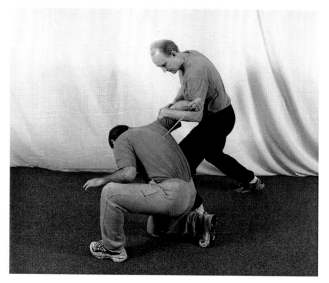

1. When Black perceives the attack, he has no time to move out of the way. Turning to cover with two hands is awkward and time-consuming, so he strikes away Gray's thrust.

2. Black does not pull his hand back after the strike. Instead, he snakes it inside, under, and around Gray's arm to trap it in the under bind.

3. At the same time, Black pivots clockwise to obtain the lower key lock.

4. Black finishes Gray with a blow to the back of the neck (not shown).

Hock Hochheim advocates a similar cover.[13]

Cover with the Straight Hand
Source: Meyer

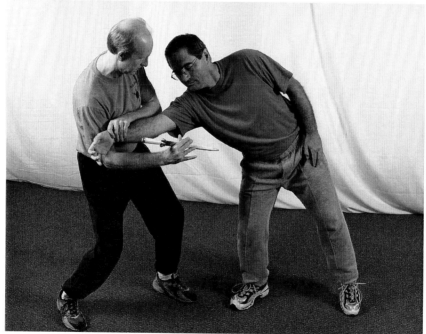

1. Gray thrusts from below. The attack came as a surprise and Black's hands are down and on the outside of the line of attack, so he covers using Meyer's "straight hand." Black pivots as he performs the cover to get his body out of the way of the blow.

2. Once Black has secured the arm, he takes the dagger by placing his hand on the top of the

blade and rotating the blade along the plane of Gray's forearm toward the elbow.

Although Meyer describes a dagger-taking after this cover, you can instead apply any number of other techniques. This cover leads naturally, for instance, to the armpit lock simply by adding a clockwise turn.

SECTION IV: DEFENSES EXPLOITING THE OFF ARM

Attackers may extend the off arm (the non-weapon-bearing hand) as they approach—sometimes to push the victim or grab the collar or the hair. Defenses involving an attack of the off arm are important and effective, as modern experience demonstrates. LaFond reports this story of a successful modern knife defense against the off arm. The protagonist is a jujutsu practitioner and the bad guy is a would-be shoplifter:

Rich, a supermarket manager and jujustu stylist, grabbed a greedy biker wannabe from the left side. The punk drew a folder from his right pants pocket (probably the front). Rich did not see the blade. But upon hearing the click of the blade lock, he said to himself, "Oh, [$#!%]!" He applied an arm bar and pressed the knifer's chest to the pavement.[14]

Medieval and Renaissance artwork often shows dagger (and sword) attacks in conjunction with a grab of either the hair or the lapel. This type of assault was evidently common. Consequently, the masters developed techniques to counter this tactic, even though Fiore believed, "a grab to the collar is not very effective because of the damage I will inflict on your elbow."[15]

Below is an armpit trap, followed by techniques that specifically address the lapel grab. Some of them can be employed to defeat a hair grab or a choke.

Armpit Trap against the Off Arm
Source: Cynner, Meyer

 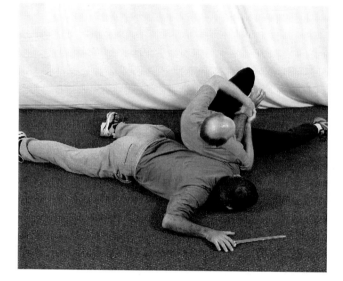

1. Gray leads his attack with his right arm extended before him, intending to push Black off balance, grab him, or otherwise frustrate an expected countermove.

2. Instead of performing a cover against the dagger arm, Black catches Gray's left forearm with his left reverse hand.

3. Black pivots, throws his right arm over Gray's, and traps Gray's elbow in his armpit. He

locks down and sends Gray to the ground, where he breaks Gray's arm.

Many of the locks previously demonstrated can be effectively used against the off arm. The pressing armlock (often called the "arm bar") is particularly effective, as Rich's experience proves.

Elbow Smash
Source: Fiore

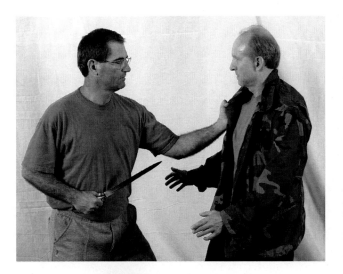

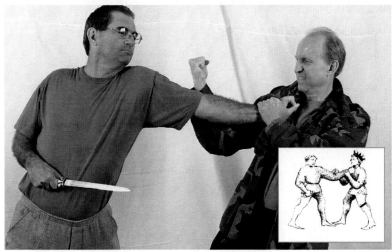

1. Gray begins his attack by grabbing Black's lapel with his left hand, dagger threatening in the right.

2. Black pulls back to extend Gray's arm.

3. When Gray's arm is extended, it is vulnerable to a blow to the elbow, which Black delivers with his forearm.

With a strong hit to Gray's elbow, the damage to his arm can be so great that the encounter is over and no follow-up is needed. However, when you perform any lapel break, you should have a follow-up technique in mind because most such defenses are only the beginning of the defense. You must then rely on one of the other defenses shown above.

This technique requires the full, or nearly full, extension of Gray's arm, which is why it is shown with Black pulling back. It can be usefully employed if Gray is pushing Black away as well. If Gray is pulling Black toward him, however, it is unlikely that Black will succeed in causing Gray's arm to extend. Thus, in that situation, another technique is called for.

Breaking Loose
Source: Fiore

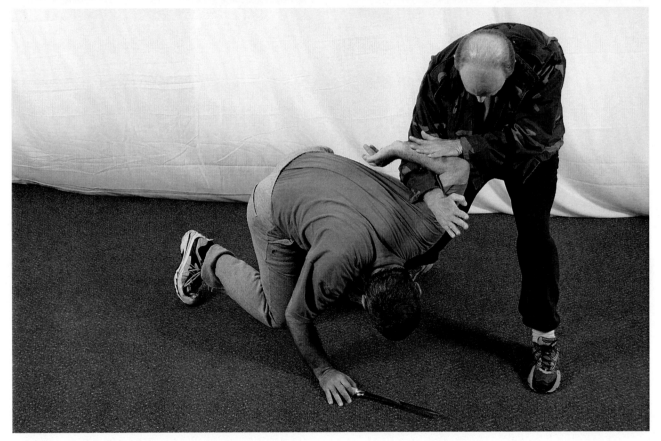

1. Gray grasps Black's lapel and pulls him forward in preparation for a stab. Black sees that Gray's arm will not straighten so there is no opportunity to call on one of the techniques attacking the elbow, such as the one shown before.

2. Black raises his arm and strikes forcefully with his elbow on Gray's forearm as close to the wrist as he can.

3. This elbow strike dislodges Gray's grip.

4. Black continues by circling his arm beneath Gray's to achieve an under bind and the low key.

113

Wiping Away
Source: Fiore

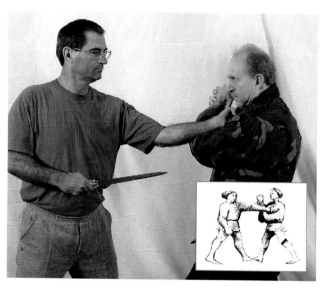

1. Again, Gray grasps Black's lapel and pulls him forward into an incoming stab.

2. Black grasps his left fist or wrist with his right hand and forcefully sweeps his supported left forearm against Gray's behind the wrist.

3. Black then grasps Gray's forearm with his left hand and applies a pressing armlock by driving his right forearm onto Gray's elbow while pulling up sharply with his left hand.

Black's follow-up technique must be decisive, whatever form it takes. Here, he should either smash the elbow joint, breaking it, or drive Gray face first into the ground. Black cannot afford to remain standing in place. Otherwise Gray will escape or stab Black in the legs or lower body.

Wiping away is effective even against a very strong grip. It defeats all chokes from the front, including the popular judo scissors collar choke.

Twisting Down
Source: Fiore

1. Gray grabs and Black immediately countergrabs, placing his left hand on Gray's wrist and his right hand on Gray's elbow. It does not matter whether Gray's arm is extended or bent, although it is better if the arm is extended.

2. Black pushes up with his right hand on the elbow and down on the wrist with his left hand. This creates pressure on Gray's elbow. At the same time, Black pivots 180 degrees so that he and Gray are facing in the same direction. This press and turn results in the pressing armlock.

I favor achieving the pressing armlock or arm bar by using a pivoting or turning action as the most efficient means of bringing Gray down, although the same armlock can be obtained by driving toward Black's left while applying pressure to the arm. But in this situation, where Gray threatens with a dagger in his right hand, the turning action takes Black out of range of the dagger.

Catching the Arm
Source: Fiore

 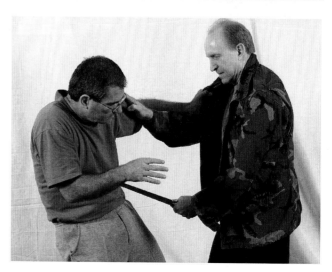

1. Gray's attack with the dagger comes too quickly for Black to work against Gray's left arm and hand, which grasps the collar.

2. Although Black's situation is desperate, he is not without a remedy. Here, he covers Gray's attack by using a two-hand grasp of Gray's dagger arm just as he would if Gray had not grabbed his collar.

3. Black then takes the dagger by placing his right palm on the top of the blade as close to the point as he can safely manage.

4. Black pushes the dagger's point toward Gray's elbow, making sure that he does so along the same plane as Gray's forearm, forcing the dagger out of the gap between Gray's palm and little finger.

5. Black switches the dagger to his left hand and returns the favor.

SECTION IV: BLOWS AND THE DAGGER

Although Talhoffer's 1459 manual illustrates combining the cover with a blow, he does not describe what to do after the blow has landed. This leaves open the possibility that he intended blows to be combined with wrestling, so that in this example, Black could follow with any of the wrestling techniques illustrated above. Covering, striking, and locking, by coincidence, is the method of unarmed knife defense advocated by Hock Hochheim.

There is evidence that medieval and Renaissance men used a punch in which the fist connected with the thumb up, which is known as the standing fist in some Asian systems. Here we have chosen to illustrate a blow taken from pankration. Ancient statues depicting pankration show the punch delivered with the fist inverted and the thumb down. If you must hook to the head, this one of the safest ways to do it aside from hooking with the palm heel.

Cover and Hook
Source: Talhoffer (1459)

1. Gray attacks from above. Black covers with the right hand and obtains his grip.
2. Rather than responding with wrestling, Black strikes Gray in the face, here with a hook punch.

ENDNOTES

1. Sydney Anglo. *The Martial Arts of Renaissance Europe.* New Haven: Yale University Press, 2000, p. 181.
2. Bob Charron. Seminar lecture, Tampa, Florida, December 2002.
3. Hans Talhoffer. *Medieval Combat.* Mark Rector trans. Mechanicsburg, PA: Greenhill Books, 2000, plate 170. (This is the 1467 edition.)
4. Most modern knifers do not expect the victim to be armed. James LaFond. *The Logic of Steel.* Boulder, CO: Paladin Press, 2001, p. 88.
5. Ibid., p. 26. LaFond surveyed more than 1,000 violent incidents in Baltimore and concluded that "the most common type of armed encounter was with a knife or knife-like weapon, not the firearm as the experts would have us believe."
6. Harold Peterson. *Daggers and Fighting Knives of the Western World: From the Stone Age till 1900.* New York: Walker & Company, 1968, p. 12.
7. Ibid., p. 15.
8. Christopher Caile. "Defeating a Downward Knife Stab," www.fightingarts.com/reading/article.php?id =364. Caile describes being attacked by a mentally disturbed man who used a thrust from above. He defeated this surprise attack using a cover described in this book.
9. LaFond, p. 22.
10. According to LaFond, 86 percent of knife attacks in his study of 275 incidents involved the forward thrust. Ibid., p. 22.
11. Filippo Vadi. *Arte Gladiatoria Dimicandi.* Luca Porzio and Gregory Mele trans. Union City, CA: Chivalry Bookshelf, 2002, p. 153, shows the straight thrust from below executed without a passing step, while on p. 154, the attack is shown with a passing step.
12. Fabian von Auerswald. *Ringer Kunst.* Wittenberg, Germany: Hans Lufft, 1539.
13. W. Hock Hochheim. *Knife Fighting Encyclopedia, Vol. 1.* Ft. Oglethorpe, GA: Lauric Press, 2000, p. 175.
14. LaFond, p. 156. On page 155, LaFond also illustrates the use of a lower key bind to secure a knifer's off arm. The technique is similar to one found in the medieval and Renaissance manuals.
15. Fiore de Liberi, Hermes Michelini transl. (Pisani-Dossi version, www.varmouries.com/wildrose/fiore).

CHAPTER 6

DAGGER AGAINST DAGGER

Long weapons like the sword or the halberd are powerful, frightening, and have the capacity to deal out fierce wounds. It was not unknown for swords and lances to pierce the body completely. Blows from large edged weapons could separate arms and legs from the torso, cut off the head, or cleave the skull to the collarbone, leaving the two halves to fall open like a split melon.[1] This makes such weapons especially respected and, in the case of the sword, the progenitor of an almost cultlike reverence. But the medieval and Renaissance masters had a realistic appreciation for the capacities of the weapons they faced and wielded, and they feared and respected short weapons such as the dagger even more than long ones. As Antonio Manciolino, an Italian fencing master, wrote in 1531:

When the weapons are too short, they are said to be as much more dangerous, because that which offends at closer distance is of greater peril, since such blows, through arriving immediately, cannot be warded; from which it follows that the partisan carries more danger than the lance, and the dagger moreso than the sword.[2]

Thus, the confrontation of men armed only with daggers was especially feared because of the speed with which blows could be delivered and the consequent difficulty in defending against them.

Nevertheless, the masters did not shrink from the task of devising methods for dagger-to-dagger combat, and substantial portions of the old manuals, particularly those written before 1500, devote considerable space to dagger play.

Like the unarmed plays, dagger-to-dagger combat as depicted in the manuals mainly addresses fighting against an opponent wielding his weapon in the reverse grip and in using the dagger in that manner. This is not to say that the masters neglected forward grip fighting, but again, as with the unarmed plays, they evidently expected the dagger to be used primarily in the reverse grip.

Modern experimentation in conditions as

realistic as can be safely achieved indicates that forward-grip fighting in a dagger-to-dagger confrontation is preferable. In a dueling environment, where both opponents are equally armed and ready, the forward grip increases the reach and allows snap cuts and stop hits while the fighter moves in and out of distance. This seems to produce a safer fight, as George Silver would put it.

However, combat is not dueling. Combat involves sudden attacks from any quarter with fully committed blows, not the feints and cautious movements of the duelist. And in combat the medieval and Renaissance masters clearly expected blades to be drawn and wielded in the reverse grip, probably because that was the way they could be deployed most quickly and could deal powerful blows that, if the enemy is armored, would penetrate mail. Thus, the masters trained their students in reverse-grip fighting as preparation for combat and practiced covers that are clearly intended for a fully committed attack of the sort that does not occur in dueling.

Although one might prefer forward-grip fighting, reverse-grip dagger combat as practiced by the Europeans deserves study by any martial artist for the depth it adds to the understanding of close combat, both historical and modern. While many of the techniques depicted in the manuals are intended for reverse-grip dagger combat, they are adaptable to fighting with short sticklike weapons, as World War II U.S. Marine Corps training materials show.[3]

Furthermore, study of the techniques depicted below will reveal how similar in principle they are to the methods of unarmed defense. In fact, most of the armed defenses can be done without a dagger in hand. You only have to substitute blows from the empty hand for blows of the dagger. This interrelationship illustrates that the medieval and Renaissance masters treated their fighting systems as integrated, with the same principles and techniques applicable regardless of the weapon being employed. They did not make artificial distinctions between unarmed and armed fighting.

THE GUARDS

Guards are positions of readiness from which to attack or defend. They involve a specific posture of the body and manner of holding and presenting the weapon—high, low, or to one side; point forward or back. Much emphasis is placed on guards in sword fencing because sword blows proceed from one guard to another; no matter how a blow is struck, the fighter ends in guard and is ready for further blows or defenses as the situation dictates. This does not mean guards are static postures. You move into and out of guards as you move with and around your opponent.

Guards also exist in dagger fencing, although most sources do not explicitly depict them. Of the few that do—Talhoffer and Meyer, for example—the guards described or illustrated resemble those in sword fencing, which by no coincidence resemble those used for staff weapons such as the spear, quarterstaff, and halberd. Common ideas ran through the old masters' approach to weapons fighting.

While guards are of paramount importance in long weapon fencing, they may have less utility in dagger play. In all likelihood the fight will develop so quickly and proceed so fluidly that neither participant will have the time to fall into a formal guard. Modern martial artist Hock Hochheim even goes as far as to reject reliance on formal guards: "so-called perfect stances so often taught are virtually impossible to maintain throughout a fight . . . I have come to the conclusion that teaching strictly enforced statue-like fighting stances is highly over-rated in true combat."[4]

Nevertheless, the dagger guards should be mastered and understood. They can be a useful starting point for mastering the techniques.

Guards have advantages in that they threaten the enemy with certain types of blows and discourage certain types of attacks, and they have disadvantages in that they can be broken by certain attacks. You must understand the strengths and weaknesses of all the guards in order to use them properly.

The most practical guards are in Talhoffer and Meyer. These are shown below.

High guard.

Shield guard.

Shield Guard

The dagger held in the shield guard is grasped in both hands, one on the grip and the other near the point. The weapon then is held at the level of the groin. This is a defensive posture and awaits the enemy's attack. Either foot can be forward.

The dagger can also be held to the side at groin level.

High Guard

In the high guard the dagger is held in reverse grip at ear level or above the head. The posture is similar to the sword guard *von tach*, or roof guard. It serves basically the same purpose: to threaten blows from above, either straight down or at an angle. The left hand can be behind the back but more often is shown resting on the left thigh (this is how Talhoffer shows it). The behind-the-back placement of the left hand and arm seems to derive from dusak and messer fencing, where it is kept back to avoid the arm cut. However, this placement will leave the left hand available for defense. Either foot can be forward.

Middle guard for reverse grip.

Middle guard for forward grip.

Middle Guard for Reverse Grip

The dagger in the middle guard for reverse grip is held at waist level near the hip. Do not extend the dagger hand. In fact, you should never extend either hand. Doing so risks a cut or a grab. Here, the left hand is on the thigh. Either foot can be forward. The principle of this guard is defense rather than attack.

Do not drop the hand so that it dangles at your side. If you do not threaten your opponent when you do this, he'll kick you in the groin for your mistake.

Middle Guard for Forward Grip

The middle guard seems to be the only guard shown in the manuals for forward-grip fighting. The dagger is held at the waist by the hip and is not extended. The left hand is generally on the left thigh. Normally, it seems the left foot is placed forward; however, the right foot can also be forward. The guard exhibits the principles of both attack and defense, since it is possible to do both from this posture without any preliminary movement, such as transitioning into another guard.

Low guard.

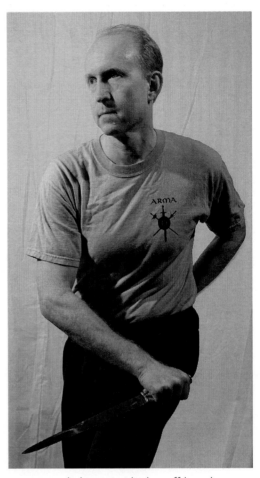

Low guard shown with the off hand
behind the back.

Low Guard

In low guard the dagger is held in reverse
grip at or below belt level with the point directed
toward the enemy. The right foot generally is
forward. The principle of this posture is defense,
although it can threaten an attack from below.

The left foot also can be advanced, and is
illustrated in Meyer in this manner, but the posture feels awkward and may be a transitional
movement.

Crossed arms.

High guard with the left hand in front of the chest.

Crossed Arms

To achieve the crossed-arm stance, the dagger is held in reverse grip with the blade along the right forearm. The right arm is over the left. Either foot can be forward. The principle of this posture is defense.

The left hand can be carried in front of the chest in any of the guards except for those requiring crossed arms. Personally, I prefer placement of the left hand on the chest. It is more readily available for defense in this position than it is on the thigh and is capable of warding blows from just about every angle. (Meyer sometimes directs the student to carry the left hand in front of the chest but does not say exactly where it should be positioned.)

Be sure not to extend the hand or arm—the damage that large knives can do to an extended arm should not be underestimated. Hock

Hochheim reports a graphic account illustrating the dangers of the extended hand in a duel involving large knives:

"The two stood off, Rai with his kukri and the Chinese with his knife. The Chinese started moving his hands in circles like a boxer, his front hand empty and open, his knife back near his chest. Rai leapt off and hit right on the front arm with that big curved blade. It [the arm] almost fell off near the elbow! But before blood could even spew, in an instant, Rai swung hard at the man's head. The end of his kukri tore into the Chinese's neck, and he fell into a human pile on the ground. I swear it was that fast. Two seconds. Two swings. Arm gone. Neck gone."[5]

Crossed shield guard.

Crossed Shield Guard

Fiore also shows a crossed shield guard. This is a posture for fighting in armor, and the defenses flowing from it do not concern us, since we are primarily interested in fighting without armor. Either foot can be forward.

The techniques that follow begin from these formal guards. However, the reader is cautioned to bear in mind that in combat the defender most likely will launch defenses and attacks without having first assumed a formal guard. Thus, the illustrations below, which can give rise to formal training patterns for pairs drill, are to some degree artificial.

SECTION I: DEFENSES FROM THE SHIELD COVER

The shield cover employs the dagger in two hands to deflect blows from above, below, and from the side. It is a universal cover that is not unique to the dagger but may be employed with any sticklike weapon against an attack by any other hand weapon. For instance, during World War II, the U.S. Marine Corps taught the shield cover with the short stick against knife, stick, and bayonet assaults.

Normally, you might expect to make a shield cover from the shield guard. This does not mean, however, that you cannot transition to a shield cover from some other posture if you need to do so. In fact, it may be preferable to start out in some other guard since standing in the shield guard may telegraph your intention to your enemy. The shield cover is intended to defeat a committed blow and is vulnerable to the feint. Moreover, you may not have had the time to assume a formal guard when the attack is launched.

Shield against the Blow from Above, No. 1
Sources: Fiore, *Gladiatoria*, Vadi, Talhoffer

1. Gray strikes from above. Black meets it with the shield cover and redirects the blow to the side.

2. Black checks Gray's arm with his left hand and stabs Gray in the body with his right.

Black's cover is not static. That is, it does not hang in the air after making contact. Rather, it meets and sweeps Gray's blow aside in a fluid movement.

I have added a check by Black's left hand to Gray's dagger arm. Checks are not illustrated or described by the medieval and Renaissance masters, so far as I am aware; however, it seems logical to check the arm to prevent any counter-movement as Black makes his counterattack.

Shield against the Blow from Above, No. 2
Source: Fiore

1. Black responds to Gray's blow from above by meeting it with the high shield and pushing Gray's arm to the right.

2. Black then grasps Gray's arm before he can withdraw it and strike again.

3. Gray is helpless to respond to Black's counterattack, a thrust from below to the body.

Shield against the Blow from Above, No. 3
Source: Fiore

1. Black meets Gray's blow from above with a shield cover that pushes Gray's arm sharply to the right.

2. Black maintains contact between his dagger and Gray's arm and pivots to follow the arm,

grasping with his left hand and seating Gray's elbow in his armpit for the armpit lock.

From here, Fiore says he can wound, break the elbow, or take the dagger.

Shield against the Blow from Below
Source: Talhoffer, Vadi, *Codex Wallerstein*, *Gladiatoria*, Meyer (for the pommel strike)

1. Gray attacks with a blow from below using the forward grip. Black covers with the low shield and redirects the blow to his left.

2. Black checks Gray's arm, strikes Gray in the face with the pommel, and counters with a stab of his own.

It seems to be critical to push the attack to the side. Talhoffer (1567) illustrates this cover without apparently pushing the blow away and shows the defender taking a wound to the stomach. Pushing the blow to the side reduces the risk of such a wound.

Shield against the Horizontal Blow
Source: Vadi, *Gladiatoria, Codex Wallerstein*

1. Gray attacks with a backhand blow toward Black's right. Black covers with the shield.

2. Black checks Gray's arm and returns the favor, here using a high thrust.

SECTION II: DEFENSES WITH THE HORIZONTAL SHIELD

There is a cover that is not usually given a specific name but which I have chosen to call the horizontal shield, after Meyer. Most sources do not specifically describe or picture how the shield should be performed. However, Meyer in several places expressly says that the dagger, held in reverse grip, should lie with the blade along the forearm. Meyer calls this the "horizontal dagger."

The *Codex Wallerstein* appears to describe the same blade placement. This type of cover is hard to do with a quillon dagger. It appears more adapted to use with the rondel or the ballock.

Other analysts, however, have interpreted this cover to employ the dagger held outward from the forearm so that it meets a blow from above as in the photo below. I will follow Meyer's instructions.

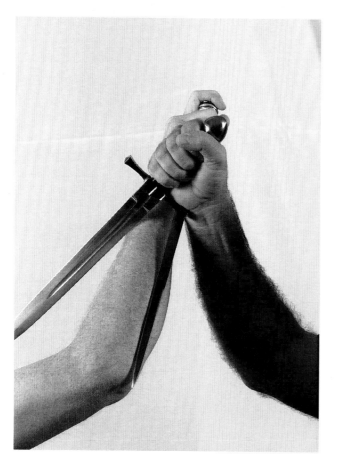

The horizontal shield.

The dagger is held outward from the forearm to meet a blow from above.

Taking the Dagger with the Horizontal Shield
Source: Talhoffer, *Codex Wallerstein*

1. Gray attacks with a blow from above. Black covers with the horizontal shield.

2. Black brings his left hand along with the shield and grasps Gray's arm to steady it.

3. At the same time, Black presses his blade up against Gray's blade. With unbroken movement, Black winds the blade of his dagger over Gray's arm so that the blade stands between Gray's forearm and the blade of Gray's dagger.

4. Black continues to wind his blade so that Gray's dagger is stripped from his grip.

The sources show the disarm without the aid of the left hand. When acting with speed and intent, I've not been able to replicate the technique without reliance on the left hand to stabilize Gray's forearm as I pry his dagger from his fingers.

SECTION III: DEFENSES WITH THE LEFT HAND AGAINST THE BLOW FROM ABOVE

Cover and Stab
Source: Talhoffer, *Gladiatoria*, Vadi

1. Black is in the middle guard with the forward grip. Gray attacks Black with a blow from above.

2. Black covers with his left hand and obtains a grip on Gray's arm.

3. Black counters with a stab to the body.

This is a simple but effective way to deal with a blow from above. Simplicity is a hallmark of medieval and Renaissance dagger techniques. The response would be the same if Black held his weapon in the reverse grip.

Upper Key, Hands Outside
Source: Talhoffer, Meyer

1. Gray attacks and Black covers with his left hand.

2. Black's cover intercepts so that Gray's arm remains bent after the cover. Black pushes the arm up and backward to maintain the bend and slips his right hand beneath Gray's upper arm.

3. Because Black holds his dagger in his right hand, he cannot grasp Gray's arm. However, with the dagger in the reverse grip, Black hooks his blade over Gray's forearm to obtain leverage.

4. Stepping deeply behind Gray's right leg, Black will forcefully drive Gray to the ground for the finish.

Take care not to place the dagger blade on your own left hand when you apply the hook.

You can precede the lock with a blow from the dagger pommel, if you like. This is not specifically described in the manuals for this upper key lock, but Meyer tells students to precede many techniques with a blow of the pommel. There is no reason why you cannot include one here.[6]

The same lock can be applied when you hold your dagger in the forward grip. Use the pommel instead of the blade to hook Gray's arm.

Break the Elbow
Source: Meyer

1. Gray is in the high guard. Black is in the middle guard. Black carries his left hand in front of his chest.

2. Gray strikes at Black's head or upper body. Black covers and catches Gray's arm on the inside behind the wrist.

3. Black redirects Gray's arm to his left. This causes the arm to straighten. Black attacks the straightened arm by striking Gray's elbow with the pommel of his dagger.

4. Black is not satisfied with the results of his blow. He decides to finish Gray with a stab, drawing his dagger to his left shoulder to deliver the counterblow to Gray's right side. The blow is made to Gray's right side because his right arm either is being held or is too damaged to perform a counter.

A sharp blow to the elbow is often enough to disable an attacker. Blows of this kind have been known to hyperextend the limb more than 45 degrees.

Backward Over-the-Leg Throw, Facing Away
Source: Meyer

 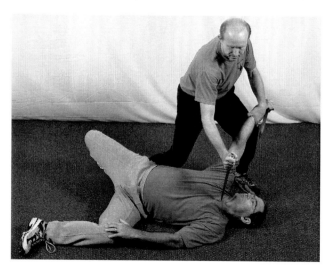

1. Gray is in the high guard. Black is in the middle guard with his left hand carried before his chest. Gray strikes at Black's head or upper body. Black intercepts Gray's arm on the inside behind the wrist.

2. As before, Black grabs the wrist and pulls Gray's arm to his left. Black strikes Gray in the face.

3. Black then steps forward, placing his right leg behind Gray's right. The hips should be touching. (Black's hip should not be behind Gray's hip.) Black continues pushing Gray in the face with the pommel of his dagger until he falls.

4. Black finishes the encounter with a stab to the chest.

Over Bind, Middle Key
Source: *Gladiatoria*

1. Black covers Gray's blow from above with an arm wrap that snakes over the top of Gray's arm and around to achieve an over bind, leading to a middle key lock exactly as if he were unarmed.

2. However, Black is not unarmed, and he responds with a counterstab of his own.

Redirect and Stab
Source: *Codex Wallerstein*

1. Black covers Gray's blow from above with a straight left hand.

2. Black redirects Gray's blow to the right and counters over Gray's arm with his own blow from above.

Black can do the same cover-and-thrust if he holds his dagger in the forward grip.

SECTION IV: DEFENSES WITH THE RIGHT HAND AGAINST THE BLOW FROM ABOVE

Pressing Arm
Source: Meyer, Talhoffer

1. Gray and Black face off in their guards. Gray is in the high guard, and Black is in the low guard.

2. Gray thrusts from above at Black's head or upper body, following the blow with a step. Black covers by thrusting his blade over the top of Gray's arm. The action is somewhat like a karate rising block (jodan uke) but lacks its

sharp focus. The action should be smooth, more of a sweeping motion of the right defensive arm. The defender should think of thrusting over Gray's arm.

3. The sweeping motion deflects the attack and turns into a pinching action, with Black capturing Gray's arm between his blade and his own forearm. At the same time, Black accompanies

the pinching action by putting his left hand on Gray's elbow.

4. Black converts the sweeping action of his right arm into a clockwise pivot toward his right. At the same time, he begins to lock Gray's arm.

5. Black completes both the pivot and the lock. The lock is accomplished by applying downward pressure with the left hand on Gray's elbow, while pulling strongly upward on Gray's wrist with Black's dagger. This action can be very painful to the wrist. Done sharply it can also result in a hyperextended elbow, what the old masters termed a *bruch*, or break. The entire defensive action is characterized by the fact that Black does not rigidly resist Gray's attack. Instead, he meets it fluidly—merges with it and redirects it. Sweeping Gray's arm, coupled with

the pivot, pulls Gray off balance and into a position where he can be easily locked up. From this position it is difficult (though not impossible) for Gray to answer effectively.

6. Here, Black drives Gray face down on the ground, the preferred finishing position for this technique. Black pins Gray by kneeling on Gray's right elbow and concludes the encounter with a stab to the neck.

During the pivot, Black must take care to finish so that his left leg is in front of Gray's right. If it is not, Gray can escape this lock.

Black can apply other locks than the pressing arm from this cover and pivot. They can lead just as well to the armpit trap or a lock in which Gray's elbow is leveraged across Black's chest or stomach.

The Scissors
Source: Talhoffer, Fiore, *Codex Wallerstein*

1. Black awaits Gray's attack in the low guard.

2. When Gray thrusts from above, Black meets it with his own counterthrust over Gray's arm to cover the blow.

3. Black pinches Gray's hand between the blade of his dagger and his forearm.

4. Black brings his left hand beneath his and Gray's arm to grasp the point of Black's dagger.

5. Having trapped Gray's arm, Black then lowers his dagger below belt level.

6. This drops Gray to his knees, where Black can deliver a finishing blow.

This defense is very painful for an unarmored enemy.

Cover, Pommel, Stab
Source: Meyer

1. Gray attacks from above.

2. Black covers with the thrust over the arm from the inside line, since his dagger hand is in that position at the start of the attack.

3. Black pinches Gray's arm between the blade of his dagger and his own forearm and redirects Gray's blow across his body to the right. He must be careful not to stab himself in the right leg as he does so.

4. When Gray's arm is extended and his blow is spent, Black checks Gray's right arm with his left hand and strikes Gray in the face with the pommel. The counterblow should travel the shortest possible path, which means directly up Gray's arm to the face.

5. The pommel strike travels through the space occupied by Gray's head and returns in a flowing, natural movement to Black's left shoulder.

6. Black then delivers the finishing blow from the left shoulder to Gray's head or neck.

Covering the Horizontal Blow with the Reverse Grip
Source: Meyer

1. Gray delivers a horizontal blow at Black's right side.

2. As Gray strikes, Black covers by thrusting over the top of Gray's arm.

3. Black pinches Gray's arm between his blade and forearm.

4. Black redirects Gray's arm downward and across his body to his left, careful not to be stabbed by either dagger.

5. Black strikes Gray in the face with the pommel.

6. Black finishes with a blow to the neck.

Cover and Stab
Source: Talhoffer

1. Black's blade is down when Gray attacks from above, only this time Black holds his dagger in the forward grip.

2. Black covers with his right forearm.

3. Since Black's right hand is unable to obtain a grip, he pushes Gray's arm to the side.

4. When Gray's arm is displaced, Black checks with his left hand and counterthrusts with his dagger.

Cover and the Short Hip (Forward Over-the-Leg Throw)
Source: Talhoffer

1. Holding his dagger in the forward grip, Black covers Gray's attack with his right forearm and pushes Gray's arm right and down.

2. Black clasps Gray's dagger arm and steps across the front of Gray's body with his left leg outstretched while encircling Gray's head with his left arm.

3. Black then throws Gray across his out-stretched leg and finishes with a stab of his own while Gray lies momentarily helpless from the fall.

Talhoffer describes this throw as a hip throw, rather than the short hip, as shown here. It can be done both ways. The technique can also be done when Black holds his dagger in the reverse grip.

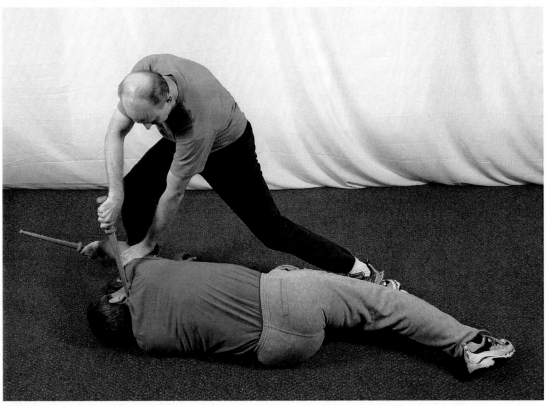

SECTION V: DEFENSES FROM THE COVER WITH TWO HANDS AGAINST THE THRUST FROM BELOW

Over-the-Shoulder Break

Source: Meyer, Talhoffer

1. Gray attacks with a thrust from below.

2. Black covers with both hands. Care must be taken to ensure that the heel of his left hand is on the top of Gray's forearm, as in the unarmed cover. Black's blade takes the place of the heel of his right hand and supports the left hand.

3. Black jerks Gray's arm forcefully forward and down, then pivots clockwise toward his right so that he and Gray end up back-to-back. At the same time, Black raises Gray's arm so Gray's elbow rests on Black's left shoulder.

4. Black completes the defense by breaking Gray's arm.

Here Black holds his dagger in the reverse grip, but the defense is the same with the forward grip. Use the blade to support the left hand.

Cover, Pommel, Stab
Source: Meyer

1. Gray attacks with the thrust from below and Black covers as before, supporting his empty left hand with the dagger blade in his right.

2. From the cover, Black immediately thrusts the pommel into Gray's face.

3. Black finishes with his own counterblow from above.

Crossed Arms
Source: Meyer

1. Black meets Gray's thrust from below with crossed arms, his own dagger lying along his forearm.

2. As soon as their arms touch, Black pushes Gray's arm to the left with his left hand, trying to obtain a grip but maintaining contact if he cannot. He draws back his dagger to strike.

3. Black completes the strike from below to Gray's body.

SECTION VI: DEFENSES WITH TWO HANDS AGAINST THE BLOW FROM ABOVE

Crossed Hands and Stab from Above
Source: Meyer

1. Black meets Gray's thrust from below with crossed hands.

2. Maintaining contact with Gray's dagger hand with his left, Black draws his dagger back to the shoulder.

3. Black strikes Gray in the neck.

Black counterattacks from above because when he covers, his right hand (which holds his weapon) is on top of his left. If Black's right hand were below his left in the cover, he would respond with a horizontal blow to Gray's body.

SECTION VII: DEFENSES FROM THE COVER WITH THE LEFT HAND AGAINST THE THRUST FROM BELOW

Striking Away
Source: Kal, Solothurner fight book

1. When Gray attacks from below, Black strikes the inside of Gray's forearm with the edge of his hand.

2. Immediately after striking away, Black delivers his counterthrust.

163

One-Hand Grasp
Source: Vadi

1. When Gray attacks from below, Black covers by catching Gray's hand behind the wrist. The action is similar to the cover with two hands. Be sure that the heel of your left hand is on top of Gray's forearm. If it is not, you may not be able to interrupt the momentum of Gray's blow.

2. When Black obtains his grip, he follows with a counterthrust.

It is not clear from Vadi's manuscript that he intends the cover to be made with one hand alone. He could have meant this to be a cover with the left hand to be supported by the dagger blade. However, I have chosen to interpret the cover as a one-handed defense. It is possible to intercept and catch the attacker's arm in this manner, even when the blow is made at full power and speed. The danger is that this cover is not as reliable as the two-handed cover. But you do not always have the ability to perform the safest cover. You must do what you can, and sometimes that involves reliance on only a one-handed cover.

SECTION VIII: DEFENSES FROM THE COVER WITH THE RIGHT HAND AGAINST THE THRUST FROM BELOW

Striking Away
Source: Talhoffer

1. Black confronts a sudden attack from his right side. Both men are in the forward grip.

2. Gray thrusts from below.

3. Black strikes away Gray's blow.

4. With Gray's arm temporarily displaced, he

is vulnerable to Black's immediate counterthrust.

Having the hand in the forward grip is not a prerequisite to using this cover. Black can strike away a blow from below while gripping his dagger in the reverse grip.

SECTION IX: THE HAND CUT

Counterthrust
Source: Vadi

1. Black is in the shield guard.

2. Gray attacks with a thrust from below.

3. Black responds by counterthrusting at Gray's hand.

Fiore shows this counter against a blow from above. He also illustrates it with one hand holding the grip and the other the blade. He says in the Getty manuscript that it is meant more for fighting in armor, where the attack is to the relatively undefended palm of the gloved hand.

Classic Hand Cut against the Thrust from Below
Source: Kal, Solothurner fight book

1. Black and Gray prepare to duel, both in the forward grip.

2. Gray thrusts from below.

3. Black avoids the thrust and countercuts Gray's arm or hand.

Classic Hand Cut against the Thrust from Above
Source: Kal, Solothurner fight book

1. Black and Gray prepare to duel. Black is in the forward grip, Gray is in the reverse grip.

2. Gray attacks with a blow from above.

3. Black cuts at the underside of Gray's hand or forearm.

Most people who have studied Kal and the Solothurner fight book interpret this move as a hand cut. But there is an alternative interpretation. The move may be a set aside of the forearm with the blade of the dagger. It is possible to set aside even strong blows if they are met near the dagger's cross and the blade is at a sharp angle to the path of the attack. Like other such covers, the action is a fluid meet-and-sweep-aside movement. Once the blow is set aside, it is a simple thing to respond with a counterthrust of your own.

A definitive explanation awaits the translation of the Kal text.

SECTION X: SELECTED COUNTERS

Every technique has its counters, which a fighter must be prepared either to execute or to frustrate. Here are three selected counters to techniques shown above.

Counter to the Upper Key Bind
Source: Fiore

1. Gray obtains an upper key bind with both hands outside Black's arm.

2. Black counters the bind by grasping his captive right hand with his left and pushes his right arm against the bind.

The principle illustrated in this counter can be used to frustrate any of the key locks. It does not matter how Gray holds Black's arm to obtain the lock.

Counter to Pressing Arm/Arm Bar
Source: Talhoffer

1. Gray obtains the pressing arm bar but he makes a mistake: he does not place his left leg in front of Black's right leg.

2. This failure opens a door through which Black can escape from the bind, and he takes it by pivoting as shown.

3. By pivoting, Black loads Gray on his left hip and throws him.

4. Gray lands behind Black, who continues his turning movement and finishes the engagement by stabbing Gray while he lies momentarily helpless.

Black's pivot must be a smooth, continuous motion. If he hesitates for even the slightest instant, Gray will extricate himself from the throw. Small men can bring down larger men with this throw.

Escape from the Scissors
Source: Kal

1. Gray gets a scissors hold on Black's right arm.

2. Although this is a very painful hold, Black does not submit. Instead, he shifts his dagger to his left hand and counterattacks.

This technique illustrates an important principle: When your dagger arm is bound or grasped, switch the weapon to the free hand. This usually enables you to neutralize the bind, whatever it is, and continue the attack. The ability to switch the dagger to the free hand is one of the things that makes fighting on the ground with a dagger extremely dangerous. On the ground, when the dagger arm is bound or tied up in some way, it is often a simple thing to switch hands. Because the switch occurs so quickly, there is almost no defense available to the enemy.

SECTION XI: HOW TO ATTACK

Reverse Grip, Feint High, Stab Low
Source: *Codex Wallerstein*, Meyer

1. Threatening in the high guard, Black approaches Gray.

2. Black feints a thrust from above.

3. If Gray responds to the feint, Black shifts his attack and makes a reverse-grip thrust from below.

The movement of the feint is exaggerated for purposes of these photos.

Forward Grip, Feint High, Stab Low
Source: Meyer

1. Holding in the forward grip, Black approaches Gray, who is also in the forward grip.

2. Black feints a high thrust at Gray's head or neck.

3. If Gray rises to the bait and attempts a cover, Black promptly changes his line of attack to a thrust from below.

The attack is the same regardless of Gray's grip.

Forward Grip, Feint Low, Stab High
Source: Meyer

1. Holding in the forward grip, Black advances on Gray.

2. Black feints a low thrust and when Gray tries to cover, Black changes his line of attack to a high thrust.

The principle applies to feints and attacks on any combination of lines, so you could also feint a hook to the body or head and thrust somewhere else. Be creative.

Continuous Attack, High-High
Source: Extrapolation from Meyer

1. Black is in the reverse grip and Gray is in the forward grip.

2. Black attacks from his right with a thrust from above.

3. When Black sees Gray's attempt to cover, he changes the line of attack by bringing his dagger down and across his body to his left shoulder.

4. Black thrusts over the top of Gray's right arm at Gray's face of neck.

Meyer does not explain why you would attack continuously in this manner. It seems like a risky thing to do because of the possibility that the opponent could counterthrust in the interval between the first and second strike, in what medieval and Renaissance German swordsmen called the *nach*, or after. This technique may draw on advice given by 14th-century swordsman Hanko Döbringer. He advised being first to strike to an opening and then striking immediately to another opening. He called this "winning the first strike and winning the after strike." Repeating the teachings of his master, Johannes Liechtenauer, the leading German swordsman of the 14th century, Döbringer argued that powerful multiple strikes would confuse the enemy and he would be unable to respond to them:

he [Liechtenauer] means that you with a good first strike shall close in without fear or hesitation and strike at the openings, to the head and to the body, regardless whether you hit or miss you will confuse the opponent and put fear into him, so that he does not know what to do against you. Then before the opponent can gather himself and come back, you shall do the after strike so that he will have to defend yet again and not be able to strike himself. Thus when you strike the first strike and the opponent defends against this, in the defence you will always be first to reach the after strike before the opponent.[7]

Continuous Attack, High-Low-High
Source: Meyer

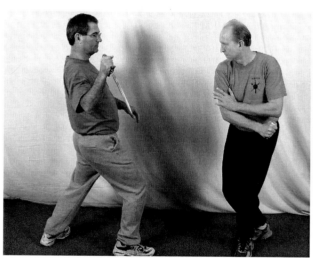

1. Black and Gray are both in the reverse grip.

2. Black attacks from his right with a thrust from above.

3. Black misses his hit as Gray retreats out of range.

4. Black does not pause in his attack and strikes an upward backhand blow from his left.

5. Black ends the thrust from below in the high guard, with the dagger at his right shoulder.

6. Black continues the attack with a thrust from above delivered from his right, which in this case finds a target.

ENDNOTES

1. J. Christoph Amberger. *The Secret History of the Sword*. Burbank, CA: Unique Publications, 1996, pp. 21–23, 39–40, 105–107.

2. Antonio Manciolino. *Nova Opera* (1531). W. Jherek Swanger, trans., www.drizzle.com/~celyn/jherek/EngManc.pdf.

3. U.S. Marine Corps. *The USMC Combat Conditioning Series: Bayonet, Club, and Knife Fighting*. Boulder, CO: Paladin Press, 2004.

4. Hock Hochheim. *Military Knife Combat*. Ft. Oglethorpe, GA: Lauric Press, p. 14.

5. Hochheim, p. 59.

6. The same technique is illustrated in Hochheim, p. 127.

7. Hanko Döbringer. *Codex HS 3227a or Hanko Döbringer fechtbuch from 1389*. David Lindholm, trans., www.thearma.org/Manuals/dobringer.html., p. 18.

CHAPTER 7

THE DAGGER FIGHT
ACCORDING TO SILVER

George Silver's method of dagger fighting differs markedly from that advocated by other medieval and Renaissance masters whose works survive. To understand how and why requires an appreciation for his books and the fundamental principles which underlie all close combat, regardless of the weapon, that he sets out in them.

Silver was an English gentleman and swordsman who lived from about 1555 to about 1622.[1] Although he was certainly highly skilled, it is open to debate whether he was technically a master of defense. (A master of defense was a martial arts teacher who was granted that status after long study and public examination by the Company of Masters, an organization recognized in 1540 and again in 1605 by the crown to regulate the teaching of martial arts in England.[2])

Silver wrote two martial arts books that we know of. The first, *Paradoxes of Defence*, was published in 1599. His second, *Brief Instructions upon my Paradoxes of Defence*, may not have been intended for publication. It remained in manuscript until it was rediscovered in 1890 and

published in 1898. The first book is largely a criticism of Italian rapier fighting, a method becoming popular in England at the time, and a defense of older, battlefield-oriented English martial arts. The second book contained brief instructions on methods of using a variety of weapons found in English martial arts, including the dagger. Both books emphasized certain fundamental concepts common to all close combat, no matter the weapon. It is thought that Silver probably did not originate these concepts. They were probably widely known and taught by English martial artists of the time. But Silver put them down on paper and preserved them for us.[3] His exposition of these principles is among the most thorough available.

Silver's instructions for the dagger-to-dagger fight are very short and general. They do not describe specific techniques, but rather an overall approach to the fight.

Of the single Dagger fyght against the lyke weapon.

1. First know yet to this weapon ther belongeth

no Wards nor gryps but against such a one
as is foolehardy & will suffer himself to haue
a ful stabb in the face or bodye to hazard
the geving of Another, then against him you
may use your left hand in throwinge him
asyde or strike up his heeles after you haue
stabbed him.

2. In this dagger fyght, you must vse conynual
motion so shal he not be able to put you to
ye cloze or grype, because your contynuall
motion disappointeth him of his true place,
& the more ferce he is in runynge in, the
sooner he gayneth you the place, wherby he
is wounded, & you not anything the rather
endangered.

3. The manner of handling your contynuall
motion is this, kepe out of distance & strike
or thrust at his hand, Arme, face or body, yet
shal press vpon you & yf he defend blow or
thrust with his dagger make you blow or
thrust at his hand.

4. Yf he com in with his left legg forewards or
with the right, do you strike at yt prte as
soon as it shalbe within your reach, remem-
bring yet you yse contynual motion in your
prgression & regressyon according to your
twyfold gournors.[4]

The archaic spelling can make the passage
hard going. But study of it rewards the reader.
Silver's dagger method revolves around general
principles and considerations rather than specific
techniques. Those considerations can be summa-
rized as:

1. There are no guards for the dagger.
2. Avoid coming to grips. Throw or trip only
when the enemy has been wounded.
3. Stay in continuous motion to prevent the
enemy from finding his "true place."
4. Stay "out of distance" while continuing to
move, and cut or thrust at any part of the
enemy's body that comes within range.

5. Avoid rushing in. He who rushes in "gains
the place" for the opponent.

For these instructions to make any sense,
however, we must understand what Silver meant
when he wrote of the "true place," "out of distance," and "gaining the place."

The true place is the spot where a man can
hit his enemy without taking a step. Your true
place is dictated by the length of your dagger
blade plus the length of your arm. Your enemy's
true place is defined by the same factors. They
are not necessarily the same distance. His arm or
weapon may be longer than yours, or vice versa.

The true place—within touching distance
with the hand—is the most dangerous place to
be. If your enemy is in his true place, it is *virtually certain that he can strike you before you
can react or defend*. It does not matter how good
you think you are, how long you have been
training, or whether you fancy yourself a grand
master and have founded your own style. If you
allow your enemy to reach his true place, you
will be hit.

"Out of distance" refers to Silver's sophisticated concept of distance. There are two types of
distance, "your distance" and "his distance."
"Your distance" is the place from which your
opponent must take a step to hit you. It does not
refer to the enemy's true place, but rather the
interval he needs to cover with one step to win
his true place. "His distance" is the converse, the
interval between you and your enemy that
includes your true place plus one step. "Out of
distance" refers to being outside of either distance. You want to remain outside your distance
as much as possible until you are ready to
attack. Being out of distance keeps you relatively
safe. Your enemy cannot hit you without moving
more than one step, which gives you time to
respond.[5]

As you can see, place and distance are related concepts. You must constantly be aware of the
distance between you and your enemy. This

requires an appreciation for the length of his reach with the weapon, your reach with your weapon, and the intervals each of you is capable of covering in a single step. That step leads to the true place. You will be trying to achieve your true place and your enemy will be trying to achieve his. At the same time, you both will be trying to deny each other the true place. By continuing to move out of distance, you frustrate your opponent's attempt to "win the place" and hit you.

In this jockeying for position, Silver advocates two habits of mind, "judgment" and "measure." Judgment is the understanding of an enemy's capabilities by the way he stands and holds his weapon and what he is able to do in consequence. Different grips and different stances confer different advantages and vulnerabilities. For instance, whether one or the other leg is forward or whether the weapon is held on one side or the other or whether it is held high or low limit the number of techniques that can be efficiently done. You must understand the advantages and limitations of every grip and stance. Measure is the calculation of keeping your space true and safe.

A primary objective in close combat is to get to the true place without being hit. Silver calls achieving the true place by your own actions "winning the place." If your enemy moves to your true place without striking first, Silver calls this "gaining the place." So, winning the place is when you achieve your true place by aggressive movement. "Gaining the place" is when your enemy moves to your true place and presents you with an opportunity for a blow, such as a stop hit.

Winning the place and distance are married to Silver's concept of "time." At its simplest, time refers to the speed at which a part of your body moves. Different parts move at different speeds. These differences have important implications in combat. Silver recognizes three types of time:

Time of the hand, the speed at which the hand moves.
Time of the body, the speed at which the body moves.
Time of the foot or feet, the speed at which the foot or feet move.

Consideration of the speed of movement for parts of the body dictates for Silver how one must move in combat to attack or defend. Silver divides these between *true times*, those which are proper methods of movement, and *false times*, those which are improper and will get you killed. The true times are:

Time of the hand.
Time of the hand and body.
Time of the hand, body, and foot.
Time of the hand, body, and feet.

The false times are:

Time of the foot.
Time of the foot and body.
Time of the foot, body, and hand.
Time of the feet, body, and hand.

Time of the hand is the most important. Silver explicitly states that in the attack, the *hand moves before the foot*:

The true fights be these: whatsoeuer is done with the hand before the foot or feet is true fight. The false fights be these: whatsoeuer is done with the foot or feet before the hand, is false, because the hand is swifter then the foot, the foot or feet being a slower mouer then the hand: the hand in that maner of fight is tied to the time of the foot or feet, and being tied thereto, hath lost his freedome, and is made thereby as

slow in his motions as the foot or feet:
and therefor that fight is false.[6]

The practical implications are enormous.
They mean that the hand moves first, followed
by the body, followed by the foot or feet. So,
when you wish to attack, you move the hand
first, then the body, and finally take a step by
moving the foot. The consequence of adhering to
this sequence means that the hand begins its
movement when you are at distance but lands
when you are in distance and at the true place
before the moving foot hits the ground.[7]

To move the foot or the body first is wrong
and invites the enemy to strike you before you
are prepared to strike him. For if you move the
foot first, you are likely to come within distance,
but since you are not in the process of striking,
you offer the enemy the opportunity to strike
first. And when the fighters are at the true place,
the first striker usually lands the first hit. In
armed fighting this is even more important than
in unarmed fighting. You may not survive a hit
in armed fighting, while you often can take a
punch or a blow in unarmed fighting.

However, it seems clear that Silver does not
intend you to attack with the dagger with full
commitment. That would be "rushing in," which
he advises against. Rather, he intends you to stay
out of distance, move continually to deny the
enemy an opportunity to win the place, and to
snipe at your enemy whenever he exposes himself, to wear him down, to watch for his mistakes
and capitalize on them. You make no attack
without being instantly ready to withdraw if
danger presents itself, what he means when he
referred to the "twyfold gournors." This fight, he
says, is "as safe and as defensive as the fight of
any other weapon."

Silver's advice, when put into practice, leads
to a fight that resembles methods advocated by
modern knife fighters, such as the approach
taught by John Styers in his book *Cold Steel*.
Styers, a student of the pre-World War II Marine

Corps close-combat expert Drexel Biddle, coun-
seled snap cuts to the arms and face and stop
hits to the face or body, not unlike Silver's
admonishment to strike or thrust at whatever
part of the enemy comes within reach.

The final question is, why does Silver advocate this kind of fight, which appears to be a far
different fight than that addressed in the other
sources? The answer is probably that Silver's
fight is a duel—a confrontation between two
equally armed men, neither of whom has surprised the other. In a duel, the cautious fight he
advocates has many significant advantages.

The fight envisioned by the other sources,
such as Fiore and Talhoffer, deals with a different situation. Fiore and Talhoffer seem
more combat oriented. The blows delivered in
Fiore and Talhoffer, as well as the other
sources, are fully committed, which means
they are not generally preceded by feints or
misdirections to confuse the victim. Committed
blows are the manner by which strikes are
delivered in combat.

ENDNOTES

1. Paul Wagner, ed. *Master of Defence: The Works of George Silver.* Boulder, CO: Paladin Press, 2003, p. 2.

2. Terry Brown. *English Martial Arts.* Norfolk, England: Anglo-Saxon Books, 1997, p. 13–37.

3. Brown, p. viii.

4. George Silver. *The Works of George Silver.* Cyril G.R. Matthey, ed. London: Bell & Sons, 1898, pp. 127–128.

5. Silver is not the only martial artist to under-stand and articulate this concept. It is known in Asian martial arts as well. In karate, prop-er distance is known as "maai." M. Nakayama. *Best Karate Vol. 1.* New York: Kodansha International, 1978, p. 16, quot-ing Minoru Miyata: "When face to face with

an opponent, the point of greatest importance in fighting strategy is distance. From a practical point of view, maai is the distance from which one can advance one step and deliver a decisive punch or kick; reciprocally, it is the distance from which [one] can withdraw one step and protect himself from attack. . . . Distancing has an important meaning in deciding victory or defeat, so it is very important to study and master advantageous maai."

6. Silver, p. 23.

7. This means that an important movement in karate is executed according to false time. In karate, many kata have a punch that is executed on a passing step. That is, the rear foot moves forward to become the lead foot. The rear hand becomes the lead hand upon this movement. After the step or simultaneously with the step, a lead hand punch is delivered. This movement is always taught with the foot moving first and the punch being withheld until the lead foot is planted or connecting when the foot lands. The punch is also delivered this way in one-step and free sparring. According to Silver, this is a false time and incorrect. The fact that this "step through punch" is never seen in karate tournaments or in full-contact karate matches is because the players have learned by hard experience that they will be hit as they execute it. This is undoubtedly because the move is always done in false time and exposes the attacker to a stop hit or kick. Karate practitioners could benefit from a study of Silver's principles.

CHAPTER 8

DAGGER AGAINST THE SWORD

Fighting with a dagger against a sword seems like a losing proposition, but sometimes men had no choice. In battle or the duel, the sword could be lost or, since swords were not habitually worn in everyday life, an affray on the street could arise in which one of the antagonists was armed with a sword and one was not. The loser was not always the man with the dagger.

Such an unequal fight occurred on the evening of July 11, 1324, with an unexpected victory for the daggerman, or maybe it's more accurate to say his survival:

> The jurors say that on the preceding Wednesday at the hour of Compline [between 8–9 p.m.] . . . Nicholas Lightfot attacked a certain Nicholas le Walsh, goldsmith, with a drawn sword in the parish of St. Mildred in the Poultry, striking him on the head so that he fell to the ground; that he immediately got up and fled towards the church of St. Benedict of Grascherche; that being pursued and pressed by the said Nicholas Lightfot, he drew his knife called a "misericord," and struck the said Nicholas on the top of his head, inflicting a fatal wound five inches long and penetrating to the brain; that the said Nicolas Flightfot so wounded returned to the Tower, where he had his ecclesiastical rights and lingered until the following Wednesday, when he died . . .[1]

Not all the manuals contain advice on what to do in this kind of unequal fight, but a few do, which give us at least some understanding about what medieval and Renaissance men might have done in such a desperate situation.

SECTION I: DAGGER AGAINST SWORD

Defense against the Cut from Above, No. 1
Source: Fiore

1. Gray menaces Black with a sword. Black has had time to deploy his dagger and he waits in the low guard.

2. Gray cuts from above at Black's head.

3. Black covers by stepping into the blow, rather than away from it, to meet the blade as close to the sword's cross as possible. The blow is weaker here than toward the point.

4. Black should angle his dagger blade steeply. If it is not angled steeply, the force of the sword blow, which can be very great even when met on the forte (the portion of the sword blade closes to the cross) as here, will drive through and strike the defender.

5. Black strikes Gray's elbow with his off hand to turn Gray.

6. Black delivers his counterblow.

Fiore's drawings of this technique can give the impression that he may intend the dagger blade to lie along the forearm rather than being extended at an angle, as I have chosen to show. I have decided on this interpretation based on experiments in freeplay. Covering with the blade extended as shown here will work. An interpretation that places the dagger along the forearm results in a cover too close to the head for my comfort. You can try it either way and see which works better for you.

Defense against the Cut from Above, No. 2
Source: *Gladiatoria*

1. Gray menaces Black, who waits in the shield guard.

2. Gray delivers a blow to the head, and Black moves into the blow to meet it. In this example, the blow is delivered at 12 o'clock, or straight downward. Black moves into the blow and answers with a high shield. Black is careful to take the blow on the flat of his dagger. If he takes it on an edge, his own blade will be driven into his palm by the force of the blow. This can be very painful, especially if the dagger is sharpened on both edges, and it could cause Black to drop his dagger.

3. The high shield block is not a static defense. You don't put it up and hold it there like a statue. Like all dagger defenses, the high shield is fluid, in which one movement melds seamlessly with the next. Here, Black sweeps the blade to his right. This sweep must be performed as soon as the blades make contact. There must be no pause between the shield and the sweep. They are, in fact, one movement.

4. Black has directed Gray's sword to the ground. Here, he momentarily pins the sword to the ground with the blade of his dagger while checking Gray's leading arm.

5. Black finishes with a thrust to the throat while continuing his check on Gray's arm.

Defense against the Cut from Above, No. 3
Source: extrapolation from Durer

1. Gray prepares to attack Black, who waits in the middle guard holding his dagger in the forward grip.

2. When Gray attacks, Black strikes Gray's sword aside, moving to the left as he does so.

3. With Gray's blade deflected, he is vulnerable to Black's counterattack. Black checks Gray's arm to prevent a false edge cut from below, and thrusts at Gray's neck.

Durer shows this cover, but he does not show the counterattack.

Defense against the Thrust, No. 1
Source: Fiore

1. Gray lies in the middle guard of Italian longsword fencing (*posta breve*). From this position, the quickest attack is the thrust. Black anticipates the thrust because of Gray's lie, and waits in the low guard with reverse grip.

2. When Gray attacks, Black sets aside the thrust with his dagger by sweeping it across the path of the thrust to deflect his enemy's blade. It should not take much force to make the deflection. Speed rather than force should be the order of the day.

3. After deflecting the thrust, Black pushes Gray on the elbow to turn him and delivers his counterattack.

Defense against the Thrust, No. 2
Source: extrapolation from Durer

1. Gray lies in the German longsword guard *pflug*, or plow. Black waits in middle guard for dagger with reverse grip.

2. Gray attacks and Black covers by deflecting the sword with his dagger to his left. Here he grasps Gray's sword to prevent any further movement by Gray.

3. Black counters with a backhand blow to Gray's chest.

Durer shows this cover, but he does not describe what to do afterward.

The covers against the thrust can also be performed with the forward grip as well, although to my knowledge such covers are not shown in the manuals outside of two-weapon, sword-and-dagger combat.

CHALLENGES OF FACING THE SWORD

Experiments in full-contact freeplay have revealed that fighting with the dagger against the sword can be a real challenge. Defending against cuts to the legs is especially hard. The best defense against cuts to the leg seems to be evasive action.

Attacks to the head are more easily dealt with, but even these are difficult to intercept. Moreover, if the swordsman has any experience fighting a man with a dagger, he will precede his attack with a feint to draw out a defense and make his real attack elsewhere, which usually connects. Analysis of videos of full-contact fights between sword and dagger indicate that the experienced swordsman who fakes a blow from above and cuts to the leg or body often makes contact with the forte of the sword due to the dagger man's forward rush to get under the initial blow. Blows with the forte are relatively weak and may not result in debilitating injury or the immediate death or incapacitation of the dagger man, who is then in a position to stab the swordsman despite his wound.[2]

However, if the swordsman is unused to facing a dagger man, he often will be overconfident. This usually leads the swordsman to make a fully committed attack to the head, and it is this attack that the dagger covers seem intended to defeat.

ENDNOTES

1. Reginald R. Sharpe, ed. *Calendar of Coroners Rolls of the City of London A.D. 1300–1378.* Suffolk, England: Richard Clay and Sons, 1913, p. 90.
2. Antonio Manciolino. *Nova Opera* (1531). Swanger, W. Jherek, transl. (www.drizzle.com/~celyn/jherek/EngManc.pdf): "striking at you at close quarters he cannot harm you with that part of the sword which is from the middle back to the hilt; but it would be far worse from the middle forward."

CHAPTER 9

TRAINING

Since the 1990s there has been a surge in interest in studying medieval and Renaissance methods of combat as more manuals have become available. People from all corners of the world—Sweden, Germany, Poland, the Czech Republic, Britain, the United States, Australia, Greece, Spain, Brazil, and even Hong Kong—are rediscovering, resurrecting, and regularly training in these methods.

Why they do so is unique to each individual. Some do it to make their re-enactment experience more authentic. Others do so not as re-enactors but as serious martial artists to experience how European warriors fought with their indigenous weapons and to understand the old martial ways. Others study these methods to supplement their modern martial arts training.

Whatever reason you may have for taking up the study of medieval and Renaissance close combat, you will find the process to be as satis-

fying as the study of any other martial discipline. These methods constitute as real and authentic a martial art as can be found anywhere.

Most people are attracted to medieval and Renaissance methods because of the emphasis on the sword. This is understandable. The sword is the symbol of the warrior, and to learn something of its mysteries allows us to savor the way of the warrior. Yet, while the sword certainly is the most significant weapon employed by medieval and Renaissance men, the martial arts of the period embraced all manner of weapons, including the spear, the staff, the halberd, the bill, and the dagger, as well as the techniques of unarmed combat. The old masters saw no artificial distinction between any manner of close combat. Wrestling was considered as much a part of sword fencing as the sword itself. And the masters believed that the same principles and techniques applied from one weapon to another.

George Silver, for example, wrote that all pole weapons are handled in the same way as the two-handed sword. Having trained with the staff and the two-handed sword, I believe this to be true. There are differences between the weapons that cannot be overlooked, but there are great similarities so that if you learn one weapon well you have a foundation for the others.

While the sword and the pole weapons are alluring, the methods of dagger fighting (and dagger defense in particular) are worthy of independent study. Many of the techniques taught for other weapons have modern, real-world applicability, but none are as useful for present-day self-defense as the techniques of the dagger. Medieval and Renaissance dagger technique was invented to address the problem of the small edge weapon attack. Small edge weapons are with us still and will always be with us, regardless of efforts by the safety-first crowd to file the points off kitchen knives. If those are blunted, people will resort to other improvised weapons, as they already do. For instance, a friend of mine was attacked not long ago in a grocery store parking lot when he surprised a guy trying to break into his car. The thief tried to stab my friend with a screwdriver. Coincidentally, my friend successfully defended himself with a technique very much like one illustrated in this book.[1]

One key advantage of studying medieval and Renaissance dagger methods lies in the fact that the information in the manuals comes from the source. Many Asian systems, particularly in Japan, preserved the teachings of their founders on secret scrolls.[2] The European manuals are the equivalent of those secret scrolls, only now they are publicly available. It is as if each master was talking to us directly.

Another significant advantage is that the techniques in the manuals are real and true. By that I mean that the men who set down the techniques did so as a result of actual combat experience. For example, Fiore dei Liberi, who had been in battle

and fought duels, trained men to fight in the barriers and in battle. He, like the other masters, knew what worked in combat and sought to preserve that knowledge in a book for those who came after. The manuals are remarkably consistent: The reader finds the same techniques or variations of them from manual to manual across more than 200 years' time. "For many centuries, the fighting taught by professional masters was relevant either on the battlefield, in a formal duel or in a brawl."[3] For such techniques to be so enduring and so widely shared is an indication of their truth.

One of the problems with many modern martial arts is that, over time, techniques have crept into the art that are of questionable value in combat, the result of "great ideas" by men who had little practical fighting experience. The information in the manuals does not come to us through the filter of generations of students passing on what they had learned, perhaps imperfectly, with the risk that those teachings will be corrupted. This is especially true in knife defense. A lot of nonsense about weapons defense is being taught to students in modern systems. In fencing, techniques that look cool and may work in the training hall but don't work in combat are called "salon acquisitions." The techniques presented here, and the hundreds of others you will find if you take up exploration of the old manuals, are not salon acquisitions. They are simple techniques that have proven themselves over time and space. It is certainly telling that men separated by continental distances and many centuries derived methods of defense that are, in substance, virtually identical. For the locks and throws of *kampfringen* can be found in both Chinese and Japanese grappling systems like chin-na, fast wrestling, and koryu jujutsu. And certainly every martial artist will benefit from a study of George Silver's principles of time, place, and distance. Those principles are universal and apply in both armed and unarmed combat.

TRAINING WITH THE MASTERS

Methods of Interpretation

If you decide to enter the world of the manuals, you'll first face the challenge of interpreting them; I've tried to make that job a little easier with this book. From their own study, some may disagree with my views and may advocate doing the techniques differently. That is only natural. Reasoned disagreement and argument are the way we come to understand medieval and Renaissance combat, since we have no living teachers from the era who can instruct us, nor any unbroken chain of teachers with any preserved curriculum stretching back to that time. Only hard practice and experience with the material will show you the right way for you.

There has been considerable debate over whether you need a martial arts background before you begin your study. The medieval and Renaissance masters generally believed that you could not learn martial arts from books alone.[4] Certainly, experience in other grappling-oriented martial arts is helpful in understanding *kampfringen*, which forms the basis of dagger fighting and dagger defense. I personally have found my training in judo and aikido-style techniques to be invaluable, and I would recommend both those systems, as well as collegiate and catch-as-catch-can wrestling, chin-na, Chinese fast wrestling, koryu jujutsu, or ninpo. While you can proceed without prior martial arts experience and still master this material, I feel that having a background in a related art is helpful and assists in the avoidance of unnecessary errors.

My method of learning is to study the picture and text, attempt a reconstruction, and then compare the interpretation with how the same problem is dealt with in similar grappling systems. There is a considerable amount of similarity in the way techniques are performed—for example, the modern Western wrestling hip throw is performed much as aikidoists execute the same technique. The modern wrestling two-leg tackle or leg pick, often called a shoot, is often performed with the head in the opponent's abdomen exactly as advocated by the *Codex Wallerstein*. The sprawl defense against the shoot is also illustrated in the *Codex*. Aikido's ikkyo arm bar looks virtually identical to one of Fiore's unarmed dagger plays flowing from the cover with the right hand.

A judoka perusing the *Codex Wallerstein* and works by Auerswald and Talhoffer will see analogs to ippon seoinage, ogoshi, uki goshi,

This move advocated by Fiore varies little from aikido's ikkyo arm bar.

taiotoshi, haraigoshi, uchimata, and osotogari, as well as leg hooks and foot sweeps commonly used in competition. Thus, reference to modern grappling systems can provide insight into an ancient text and can inform an interpretation. But reference to such systems is not essential to interpretation, merely helpful. Keep an open mind.

Sometimes the ancient texts provide insight into a technique that I have not received from modern instructors and have improved my performance of the maneuver. Meyer's manuscript is notable for providing such useful missing information. Doing this study has been a tremendous learning experience.

If you can, find a more experienced person to train with and attend seminars at every opportunity. Having your interpretations critiqued by others doing the same work is invaluable and lets you know whether you're on the right track.

Training Weapons

A second concern is your training tools. Training with steel knives, even blunts, can be dangerous. I personally prefer wooden dagger replicas, known as wasters (a waster being any

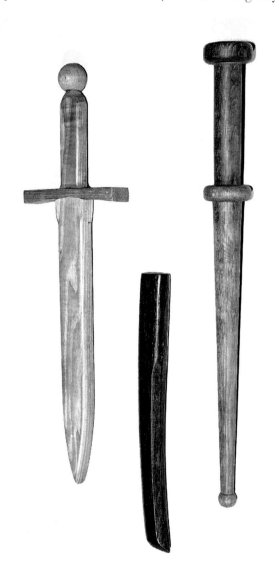

Quillon and rondel wasters pictured with widely available tanto waster.

wooden replica weapon).

From Meyer's woodcuts, it appears that the masters trained with wooden weapons, at least for dagger techniques. So there is no reason why we should not follow their example. Wasters can be bought from a variety of sources, or you can make them on a lathe. If you can't find a vendor, a wooden dowel of the appropriate length is more than satisfactory, or you can even use a commercially available tanto waster, which is shorter than Vadi's recommended length. The length of the weapon is only important for some techniques like the shield wards, which work better with a longer weapon. Remember, medieval and Renaissance men faced the possibility of dagger attack from knives of all lengths, so practicing with and against a shorter weapon is not necessarily inauthentic.

Planning for Safety

The third concern is for safety. There are risks associated with martial arts training, particularly when it involves weapons, joint locks, and throws. The harder and faster you train, the greater the risk. *Blows should not be directed at the face* unless you use some sort of face protection, such as a fencing mask or safety goggles. You don't want to lose an eye or put someone's out. Always consider face or eye protection when engaged in freeplay. When drilling, I recommend that you direct your blows to the chest rather than the face.

Care should be taken when applying the joint locks. It is easy to damage someone's elbow, and the injury can take months to heal. One guy I trained with was hurt by a heedless, overzealous training partner, and it took about nine months before his elbow was back to normal. Some techniques simply cannot be done hard or fast, such as those involving a blow to the elbow, or cannot be practiced full force. You are responsible for the safety of your training partner and must apply any technique safely, which may mean slowing it down a bit or not going all the way. Ideally you should take the lock to the point where it causes some pain to the training partner but does not damage him. When the training partner experiences pain, he should submit by tapping out, *and you should stop immediately*. Some pain is inevitable in this kind of training. You cannot know if you have correctly applied the technique if the training partner does not feel some discomfort. But remember that your partner is going to have the same chance to do the technique on you, so give only what you are willing to receive.

In this regard, it is essential that you know and trust your training partner. Some people just don't think about the harm they can do with these techniques and they lack self-control. You want to be sure that your training partner understands the duty to act responsibly. Avoid those who don't.

Because of the potential dangers, you should view training, especially in drill, as exactly that—practice. Submit to the lock and don't resist it or try to escape just to show how cool, knowledgeable, or superior you are. When you resist or try a counter, you are not helping your training partner learn the technique, because he needs to feel what it is like to get it right; your resistance will rob him of that critical perception. Moreover, when you resist in drill, your partner's inclination may be to apply more force, which could lead to injury. Freeplay is great and has its place if you both have experience and know how far you can take things, but a drill that escalates into a wrestling match can be an invitation to a trip to the hospital. Drill is an essential part of practice, and if you don't do it properly, you won't learn and progress.

When practicing the throws, here, too, the thrower is responsible for the throwee's safety. You don't want to throw the guy down hard or drop him on his head in training. Give him a soft landing by holding onto him to cushion the fall.

What goes around comes around here as well. The less you get knocked around by falling, the longer you can endure a practice session. Don't throw anybody on concrete or on a hard floor; use a mat or soft grass if you can.

The throwee must practice safety as well. The key thing is not to hit your head on the ground when you land—tuck your chin to your chest and tense your neck muscles as you land to prevent this. Fall so that you land on your side, not flat on your back or on the point of your shoulder, and don't fall on top of your arm. Don't stick your hand out to break the fall unless you want a broken wrist. Learning judo-style falling, or ukemi, is very helpful, although some people disdain it as not period appropriate (a mistake in my view; it's not period appropriate to wear face protection either, yet many do so). You might also consider acquiring forearm pads. They can shield you from forearm banging when doing some covers. And you may find elbow and knee pads useful in throwing and freeplay.

TRAINING STEPS

Interpretation of the Texts

There are four basic steps in training. First is interpretation of the texts. Even if you have an instructor, you will almost certainly turn to the texts for additional ideas. The historical texts typically illustrate a technique by a single picture, which is usually a moment frozen in time during the performance of the maneuver. Beware of trying to interpret a technique from the picture alone. Usually the picture is accompanied by a brief explanatory text. That text may describe a technique totally at odds with what you thought the picture was trying to show.

The text often does not give you step-by-step instructions but instead describes the movement in general terms. Sometimes the description is not clear and leaves room (often considerable) for disagreement about important parts of it.

201

This forces you to fill in the gaps. Try to duplicate what you believe the text and picture are trying to show. Often I start trying the maneuver solo just to get a feel for it. But you have to work it against a partner to really understand it, slowly at first, then as fast as you can safely go. If it doesn't work when you're going fast, then your interpretation is probably wrong and you have to start over.

Drill

The second step, which we've already alluded to, is drill. In my opinion, drill is the core of training. Many people don't like drill. It means repetitions—hundreds of them. It's boring. People do this stuff because they want to fight, right? So why should they be forced to do this mind-numbing drill?

You do it to master the material. There is an old saying in the Asian martial arts that you can't come to realization without pain. Its corollary is that you can't come to realization without drill. These truths are universal. The Roman army was not great by accident. Its battlefield victories rested upon its soldiers' individual skills, which were honed through drill.[5]

Only through repetition will you gain the muscle memory and a deep understanding of the techniques. If you don't drill, the technique will not become imprinted on your mind and body. You will fail to see the opportunity for a technique when it arises during freeplay. As freeplay is as close as you can safely get to combat, this means that in a real fight you will miss the main chance, which could get you killed.

There are two kinds of drill, solo and partner. You need both; they supplement each other. Solo drill, of course, you perform without a physical partner—but you should try hard to see your imaginary partner as he attacks you. Try to see and feel his attack and his reaction to your technique. Take a series of 10 or so techniques and do each one five to 10 times, working

through the series. Repeat until you've done 30–50 repetitions. Make sure you perform the movements to the air just as you would if you had a live body under your hands.

The Roman army made solo drill at the pell, a post planted in the ground, the core of infantry close-combat weapons training. Vegetius, a Roman military writer whose works were famous throughout the medieval and Renaissance periods, said of solo drill:

> We are informed by the writings of the ancients that, among their other exercises, they had that of the post. They gave their recruits round bucklers woven with willows, twice as heavy as those used in real service, and wooden swords double the weight of the common ones. They exercised them with these at the post both morning and afternoon. This is an invention of the greatest use, not only to soldiers, but also to gladiators. No man of either profession ever distinguished himself in the circus or field of battle, who was not perfect in this kind of exercise.[6]

Modern martial artists ignore this advice at their peril. The ancients followed this training regime because hard, practical experience had taught them it produced the best fighters.

For partner drills you need a live body. Here, the role of the partner, or attacker, is as important as that of the defender, which most people forget while they're doing partner drills. In traditional kenjutsu, the attacker is usually a more advanced student than the defender. There are important reasons for this: The attacker controls the pattern to be practiced by the type of technique he launches and the force and speed in which it unfolds. The attacker also is, or should be, responsible for the safety of the attack, meaning he must be in control so the blow does not injure the defender if the defense fails. Finally, the attacker must ensure that the attack is realistic, no matter what speed it takes.

This last point is very important. Many people who perform knife and dagger drills do not attack like people do in the real world. One of the most common mistakes is to attack in a pinwheeling, or pendulum, fashion, in which the arm is fully extended. I have often seen karate black belts making this foolish, elementary mistake when practicing karate's knife defenses. Real blows, however, do not travel this way: Blows from above start essentially from the ear and the arm may never be fully extended. Often it's only extended when the blade is in your body.

It is crucial that the attack in drill be realistic. If the attack follows a pinwheeling, unrealistic path, it will change your perception of the attack and how you perform your cover. If you are accustomed to seeing the attack approach in a pinwheel fashion, you may not see an attack that is made correctly. If the attacker pinwheels his arm, you can get used to covering higher than you would if he attacked correctly. Only when you understand the feeling of a realistic attack made in true time and from the true place can you have any confidence that you can defeat it. Anything less is self-deception. There is too much of that in the martial arts.

Drill for an attacker is not a passive exercise in which he shoves the waster at you while thinking, "Jeez, I can't wait until it's my turn." His mind must be as engaged in the drill as that of the defender. He must have the warrior's mindset. He must imagine that he is making a real attack. He must have the intent to do harm, even when he is executing the drill slowly or at half speed. He must perform with emotional intensity, even when he is holding back. He must be conscious of true time, place, and distance, and he must execute the attack in true time. Drill is not a one-sided affair. One of the most misunderstood

and neglected aspects of drill is that the attacker, though ultimately submitting to the defense, is training himself as well as the defender. He is not merely the defender's moving pell.

For the defender, the person performing the techniques, drill involves both physical and mental aspects as well. The physical aspects are obvious. He learns how to perform the prescribed technique. He learns the proper and most efficient way to cover and to manipulate the attacker's body. The defender learns how to move, if that is required, applying proper footwork. These are the things the instructor can see, and of which the defender is most conscious and tends to concentrate on during drill. But they are the gross, superficial aspects of drill. If you think this is what drill is all about, you are missing a great deal.

For drill, the physical, or merely technical aspects of movement and body manipulation, are just the tip of the iceberg. The mental or internal aspects of drill are just as, if not more, important. You must learn to strike truly, which means "to decide in one's mind and to carry out the resolution of intent fully."[7] It does not mean a halfhearted, floppy/sloppy execution either of the blow by the attacker or the counter by the defender. It means that when you practice blows and counters, you must, in your mind, feel as if you fully intend them to cause harm. Your mind must be as completely committed to the action as if you are in real combat, even when you ultimately are holding back.

You must be conscious of distance—how far from you is the attacker and what options do you have when he is far or near? You must be aware of the true place—what is the true place for this attacker wielding this weapon? Is he at the true place or at his distance when he launches the attack? How far do you have to move to deny him the true place, should you choose to do so, and how would you move? You must see if the attacker attacks in true time. Does he advance the foot first, moving in a false time?

Learn how to look at the opponent. Learning to see him is as important a skill as you will ever acquire. If you cannot see him properly, you cannot observe his distance and you cannot perceive an attack in time to defeat it. Nor will you become aware of proper openings for an attack of your own. There has been no consensus throughout history on the proper point of gaze.[8] Some people advise looking at his eyes, that they will telegraph his intentions because he will look at the place he is going to strike. However, I have not found that to be the case. Personally, I find it distracting to look at a man's eyes because I cannot monitor his weapons and his hands and feet when I do that. When I play karate, I place my gaze on the center of his body and then look through him, as if at an object at a distance, relying on peripheral vision to tell me what his hands and feet are doing, while concentrating on ensuring that I maintain proper distance.[9] This method works in weapons sparring as well, but I have found you have to pay more attention to the weapon carried by your opponent. With both the knife and the sword, placing the gaze on the enemy's weapon-bearing hand and monitoring the rest of him with peripheral vision seems to produce the best results, although when knife sparring I shift my gaze back and forth from his body mass to his knife arm during the flow of the encounter. This is like the method advocated by Antonio Manciolino, who advised us to watch the sword hand.[10] I hesitate to lay down hard rules on this subject, though. You should experiment and find out what works best for you. The key is to be aware of the need to develop this skill. And that starts in drill.

I do lay down one hard and fast rule, however. Never watch the weapon itself. It is as hypnotizing as the enemy's face. This is especially so when you are in a real encounter. When someone pulls a knife on you for real, your eyes will naturally be drawn to the weapon. There will be a fraction of time as you look at it and your guts curl in dread. This can produce a feeling of weakness or helplessness and a moment's hesitation that your enemy will exploit to kill you. You cannot afford that hesitation if you want to live. You must train to avoid it, and you start by not looking at the weapon itself in drill. Be aware of the dagger, for you must know its length, whether it has an edge, and whether it is single- or double-edged. But do not let your eyes linger on it.

The actual physical performance of drill starts with the base technique, which refers to the manner of executing a response to an attack as prescribed in a manual. The designation of a maneuver as a base technique is somewhat arbitrary. Most techniques, such as an armlock or throw, have many variations which turn on factors such as your or your opponent's body position at the time of the attack, whether one foot or another is forward, how you step into the technique, how you make your cover, or how or where you grasp the opponent's body. For example, take the throw known in *kampfringen* as the short hip and in judo as taiotoshi. It is characterized by pulling the opponent forward over the outstretched leg. There are at least eight different ways of gripping the opponent's upper body to accomplish this throw and at least three ways of stepping to achieve the proper foot position in relation to the opponent. This makes for at least 24 variations. You have to start somewhere, so you pick a variation and call that the base. In our study, the medieval and Renaissance masters made the selection for us. By performing the base technique, you will learn the principles behind the technique and why and how it works. Once you master the base technique, then you can consider moving on to variations.

Step 1: Start slow and perform the base technique. The attacker begins at your distance, the interval in which he has to take a step to strike you. Master the gross movements and fundamental footwork.

Step 2: As you become confident of the gross movements and footwork, work at medium to three-quarter speed.

Step 3: When you feel comfortable with the technique at three-quarter speed and can safely apply it to your training partner, go full speed with full emotional intent. This may look and feel a lot like freeplay, but it isn't.

Step 4: Vary the distance. The attacker should launch the blow at the true place without taking a step. Go back to performing the maneuver slowly and work up to full speed and intent as before.

Step 5: Explore alternatives to the base. Vary the grip or the footwork. Go back to performing slowly with each variation and work up to full speed and intent.

Step 6: Mix and match. The manuals, such as Fiore's, prescribe a single particular technique following a designated cover. Experiment by performing techniques from covers other than those prescribed in the manuals. The extrapolations illustrated above are just such experiments. Go back to performing slowly, then speed up. Vary the distance.

Step 7: Vary the angle of attack. Experiment with performing covers and techniques against attacks from the sides and from behind.

Step 8: Practice among obstacles like chairs and tables or on uneven ground, anything that inhibits your movement. Do the base, vary the distance, explore the alternatives, mix and match. If you are hit while defending, don't quit. Get used to pressing on even if you think you've been injured. If a technique fails, flow immediately into another.

This does not exhaust the creative possibilities inherent in drill. You may think of others, and more power to you. While you are performing the physical actions, you must remember to concentrate on the mental aspects as well.

Thus, drill is a multilayered exercise involving mental and physical aspects in which both players ideally are fully engaged mentally, emotionally, and physically. It is not just a tiresome exercise that you must endure until being allowed to get on to the more exciting game of freeplay.

As counterintuitive as it seems to many modern martial artists brought up in an environment where freeplay comprises the core training method, techniques learned *only* in drill can be successfully employed in combat when the pressure is on and your life is at stake. I know of a number of instances of people surviving street attacks who relied on a technique practiced only in drill. My friend attacked by the screwdriver-wielding thief never practiced his defense other than in drill. (His comment to me about the encounter was, "It was just like in class!")

Pure freeplay, or free sparring, is the unstructured exchange of techniques between players. It is a bout, practice fighting. It is an essential element of training and it should not be ignored. The Roman army recruit advanced to freeplay after mastering the fundamentals at the pell.[11] Vegetius said of this practice, "Experience even at this time convinces us that soldiers, perfect therein, are of the most service in engagements."[12]

Practice Semifreeplay

Some freeplay can be like drill and has real training value. In formal drill, the attack is prescribed so the defender knows what's coming and he makes a prescribed response. Now the choice of the attack is up to the attacker and the defender must figure out what's coming and respond appropriately with any technique that seems appropriate. The defender's responses are no more prescribed than the attacks, but the defender does not launch attacks of his own.

Unarmed defense freeplay should be more like semifreeplay than full freeplay. That is, there should be a significant limitation on the manner in which the attacker attacks. This limitation, oddly enough, is necessary to keep training realistic. If the play becomes full freeplay, the attacker inevitably will not make committed attacks and instead will resort to feints and snap cuts to deceive the unarmed defender in order to win the encounter. Knifers in the real world normally will not precede an attack with feints and snap cuts. These are the techniques of the dueling, cautious attacker, and knife attacks on the street are not duels.[13] Nor were dagger attacks of old. They are, and were, like assassinations in which the attacker relies on the suddenness and swiftness of a committed attack to surprise and overwhelm his victim. A committed attack by definition is an attack launched with the full intent that it be the sole blow and that it land and finish the enemy with that single stroke. Blows in semifreeplay—whether from above, below, or the side—should conform to this rule. Only the attacker's restraint makes this type of realistic training possible, for he must refrain from allowing the exchange to degenerate to pure freeplay.

It is important to keep this in mind when sparring the unarmed defenses, because they are designed to work against the committed attack.

Pure Freeplay

This is not to say that you should never engage in unrestricted freeplay when training the unarmed defenses. It is useful to do so, but you will find more often than not that the unarmed defender is "killed" during such engagements. This increases the more experienced the training partner becomes. However, my experience in freeplaying in this manner has been that the

medieval and Renaissance approach to knife defense has resulted in my "death" less often than when I have relied on the approaches of other systems. The benefit of full freeplay is that it hones our perceptions and reflexes like nothing else. It also shows you how vulnerable to a knife attack you are when the attacker is cautious, and how difficult it is to defend. However, even your limited success in defending against such an

If you want to freeplay against the sword, I recommend that you use a padded sparring sword specially made for freeplay. This example was made by Jeanry Chandler of New Orleans.

206

You should wear a helmet and gloves to protect your face and hands.

attack should give you confidence in the techniques.

Dagger-to-dagger freeplay can proceed to the limits you think you can safely go in the force of thrusts and the execution of techniques. This is where you hone your techniques, learn to apply them in an unrehearsed manner, and sharpen your mental skills. As mentioned, it is wise to wear safety equipment, especially face or eye protection.

As with unarmed dagger defense, you will find it very difficult to defend against an armed opponent who is experienced in facing a dagger man. Dagger defenses against weapons attacks seem to work best when the opponent launches a committed attack and does not employ feints.

Most freeplay occurs without anyone watching over the players. It is useful, however, to have a third-party observer who can critique the performances and give advice. It is also useful occasionally to videotape your performance. It's hard to remember afterward exactly what occurred during a free sparring session. In fact, sometimes your memory is not at all accurate. A videotape of a match can be very helpful in recalling precisely what happened and in spotting mistakes.

As much fun as freeplay is, there are elements that are not only a danger to your physical self but to your ability to progress as a martial artist. First, there is the danger of rushing into freeplay too soon. Some instructors like to introduce students to pure freeplay immediately. I personally think this is a mistake and that you should not begin pure freeplay until you have a grasp of the fundamentals gained through solo and partner drill. Once you have that grasp, you can safely begin testing them in freeplay. The Roman army recruit first was required to master the fundamentals through drill before he was admitted to play. The Roman master-at-arms had good reasons for this. If you begin without the necessary appreciation for the fundamentals, you will develop bad habits that will become ingrained and hard to break.

Second, you must not let freeplay become a game or a competition. When it becomes a sport, the game inevitably favors some techniques over others, which are valuable more for their tendency to gain points than for their martial soundness. These are salon techniques that the masters would never have relied on in the terrible world of combat. Tournament karate is a sad example of the degeneration that can occur in a martial art as a result of an overemphasis on sport. For example, there are few techniques as unsound as tournament karate's leaping backfist, which typically lands on a portion of the head unlikely to result in great injury. Yet, it is counted as a debilitating blow. Combat is not a game of tag and you should not let your freeplay practice degenerate to that level.

When freeplay becomes a game, there is also the possibility for the development of rules, adopted with the best intentions, that deprive the play of martial truth. Modern tournament karate often does not allow kicks to the legs, grabs, throws, and locks. Taekwon do does not allow punches to the head or kicks to the groin, and it gives premium points to kicks to encourage reliance on them. In consequence, karateka and taekwon do stylists who concentrate on winning tournaments may prepare themselves for the ring, but they prepare themselves imperfectly for combat. Other groups engage in mock armed combat and do not allow blows below the knees, grabs of either the blade or the arm, or throws. However, this results in mock combat that does not reflect real fighting, for in real fighting every part of the body is a target and every means of defeating the enemy is not only permissible but encouraged. When you disallow strikes to the legs—or to any other part of the body for that matter—count weak blows as killing ones, or eliminate grabs and throws, you change the very nature of the fight and deprive it of combat truth and real training value.

For freeplay should not be a competition, a game, or a sport, but another method of combat training that should prepare you for the Great Game: the moment when your life is at risk.

The final question is how much time to devote to solo drill, partner drill, and freeplay. The answer varies from one instructor to another in the world of martial arts and there is no consensus on the question. I personally think a quarter or less of the time should be spent performing techniques solo, at least half the time should be spent on partner drills of various kinds, and a quarter or less should be spent on freeplay. Train as hard and as realistically as it is safely possible to do.

And that is only what you do in the training hall. Your study is not limited to what takes place there. You must read the masters' works and struggle to understand what the masters were trying to tell us. And you must read all the accounts you can find about real fights and talk to people who have been in them. Read widely and think deeply.

Only in this way can you follow the true path of the warrior.

ENDNOTES

1. James LaFond devotes a chapter to such improvised stabbing weapons in his book *The Logic of Steel*, pp. 99–113.

2. See *The Sword & the Mind*, Hiroaki Sato trans. (New York: Barnes & Noble Books, 2004), the foundational scrolls for shinkage-ryu kenjutsu.
3. Sydney Anglo, *The Martial Arts of Renaissance Europe* (New Haven: Yale University Press, 2000), p. 38.
4. Anglo, p. 31–34.
5. Flavius Vegetius Renatus. "The Military Institutions of the Romans," *Roots of Strategy*. Harrisburg, PA, 1985: Stackpole Books, 1985, pp. 83–84.
6. Ibid., p. 83.
7. M. Nakayama. *Best Karate: Kumite 1*. New York: Kodansha International, 1978, p. 20, quoting Miyamoto Musashi.
8. Anglo, p. 141.
9. Nakayama, p. 16, quoting Minoru Miyata.
10. Antonio Manciolino. *Nova Opera* (1531). Swanger, W. Jherek, trans. (www.drizzle.com/~celyn/jherek/EngManc.pdf).
11. G.R. Watson. *The Roman Soldier*. Ithaca, NY: Cornell University Press, 1969, pp. 57–59. The Romans used wooden wasters for both sword and pilum, tipped with leather for safety.
12. Vegetius, p. 84.
13. LaFond includes dozens of accounts of knife attacks from assailants, victims, and witnesses in his book, *The Logic of Steel*. You will have to search hard to find one in which the knifer did not use a committed attack.

BIBLIOGRAPHY

PRIMARY SOURCES

Auerswald, Fabian von. *Ringer Kunst.* Wittenberg, Germany: Hans Lufft, 1539.

Cynner, Hans. Untitled. www.thearma.org.

Döbringer, Hanko. *Codex HS 3227a or Hanko Döbringer fechtbuch from 1389*, David Lindholm, trans. www.thearma.org/Manuals/dobringer.html.

Durer, Albrecht. *Albrecht Durer's Fechtbuch.* Friedrich Dornhoffer, ed.

Forgeng, Jeffrey. *The Medieval Art of Swordsmanship: A Facsimile and Translation of Europe's Oldest Personal Combat Treatise, Royal Armouries MS. I.33.* Union City, CA: Chivalry Bookshelf, 2003.

Kal, Paulus. Untitled, Codex CGM 1507 in the Bayerische Staatsbibliothek in Munich.

Liberi, Fiore dei. *Flos Duellatorum* (1409). Pisani-Dossi version: Hermes Michelini, trans. www.varmouries.com/wildrose/fiore; Getty version: Rob Lovett, Mark Davidson, and Mark Lancaster, trans. http://fiore.the-exiles.org; Morgan version: Eleonora Litta and Matt Easton, trans.

www.fioredeiliberi.org.

Lignitzer, Andreas. *MS 1449, the Danzig Fechbuch.* Mike Rasmusson trans. www.schielhau.org/ligniter-dagger.html.

Manciolino, Antonio. *Nova Opera* (1531). Swanger, W. Jherek, trans. www.drizzle.com/~celyn/jherek/EngManc.pdf.

Marozzo, Achille. *Arte Dell Armi.* Bologne: Antonio Pinargenti, 1568.

Meyer, Joachim. *Kunst des Fechtens.* Jeffrey Forgeng trans. Germany: 1570 (unpublished manuscript).

Silver, George. *Paradoxes of Defense.* London: Blount, 1599.

Silver, George. *The Works of George Silver.* Cyril G.R. Matthey, ed. London: Bell & Sons, 1898.

Talhoffer, Hans. *Talhoffer's Fechtbuch.* Germany: circa 1459. (Brian Hunt privately published partial translation. A third version of Talhoffer's work, dated 1443, is also available. However, as far as I know, there is no English translation for it.)

Talhoffer, Hans. *Medieval Combat.* Mark Rector trans. Mechanicsburg, PA: Greenhill Books,

2000. (This is the 1467 version of the Talhoffer manuscript.)

Unknown. *The Codex Wallerstein.* Grzegorz Zabinski and Barolomeij Walczak trans. Boulder, CO: Paladin Press, 2002.

Unknown. *Gladiatoria.* Jeffery Forgeng trans. Germany: circa 1450. (Unpublished manuscript.)

Unknown. *The Solothurner Fechtbuch.* Germany: circa 1500. www.thearma.org.

Vadi, Filippo. *Arte Gladiatoria Dimicandi.* Luca Porzio and Gregory Mele trans. Union City, CA: Chivalry Bookshelf, 2002.

SECONDARY SOURCES (BOOKS)

Abwehr Englischer Gangster-Methoden. Norway: P.K. DES A.O.K., 1942.

Amberger, J. Christoph. *The Secret History of the Sword.* Burbank, CA: Unique Publications, 1996.

Anglo, Sydney. *The Martial Arts of Renaissance Europe.* New Haven: Yale University Press, 2000.

Applegate, Rex. *Kill or Get Killed.* Boulder, CO: Paladin Press, 1976.

Ben-Asher, David. *Fighting Fit: The Israeli Defense Forces Guide to Physical Fitness and Self-Defense.* New York: Putnam, 1983.

Boardman, Andrew W. *The Medieval Soldier in the Wars of the Roses.* Stroud, Great Britain: Sutton Publishing, 1999.

Brown, Terry. *English Martial Arts.* Norfolk, England: Anglo-Saxon Books, 1997.

Burns, Farmer. *Lessons in Wrestling and Physical Culture.* Tampa, FL: Matt Furey Enterprises, 2002.

Caile, Christopher. "Defeating a Downward Knife Stab," www.fightingarts.com/ reading/article.php?id

Carter, Michael. *Basics of German Longsword according to Joachim Meyer.* 2005. (Unpublished manuscript.)

Cartmell, Tim. *Effortless Combat Throws.* Burbank, CA: Unique Publications, 1999.

Cassidy, William L. *The Complete Book of Knife Fighting.* Boulder, CO: Paladin Press, 1975.

Christensen, Loren W. *Fighter's Factbook.* Wethersfield, CT: Turtle Press, 2000.

Clements, John. *Renaissance Swordsmanship.* Boulder, CO: Paladin Press, 1997.

Clements, John. *Medieval Swordsmanship.* Boulder, CO: Paladin Press, 1998.

Clements, John. *Top Myths of Renaissance Martial Arts.* (Association for Renaissance Martial Arts, www.thearma.org/essays/ TopMyths.htm, undated).

Clements, John. *The Art of Well Meaning Error* (Association for Renaissance Martial Arts, www.thearma.org/essays/barbasetti .htm, undated).

Clements, John. *Core Assumptions and the Exploration of Historical Fencing.* (Association for Renaissance Martial Arts, www.thearma.org/essays/core_assumptions.h tml, undated).

Clements, John. *The Source Manuals: Some Thoughts on the Problems of Interpretation and Application* (Association for Renaissance Martial Arts, www.thearma.org/essays/ interandapp.htm, undated).

Clements, John, and Hertz, Brenda. *The Myth of Thrusting versus Cutting Swords* (Association for Renaissance Martial Arts, www.thearma .org/essays/thrusting_vs_cutting.html, undated).

Dean, Bashford. *Catalogue of European Daggers 1300–1800.* New York: Metropolitan Museum of Art, 1929.

Easton, Matt. Untitled biography of Fiore dei Liberi. www.fioredeiliberi.org/fiore/

Echanis, Michael D. *Special Forces Ranger-UDT/Seal Hand-to-Hand Combat/Special Weapons/Special Tactics: Knife Self-Defense for Combat.* Burbank, CA: Ohara Publications, 1977.

BIBLIOGRAPHY

Embleton, Gerry. *Medieval Military Costume.* Wiltshire, England: Crown Press, 2000.

Embleton, Gerry, and Howe, John. *The Medieval Soldier.* London: Windrow & Greene, 1994.

Eyrbriggja Saga ch. 58, William Short, trans. excerpt at www.hurstwic.org/library/ arms_in_sagas

Goldsworthy, Adrian. *Roman Warfare.* London: Cassell, 2000.

Gravett, Christopher, and Turner, Graham. *English Medieval Knight 1300–1400.* Oxford: Osprey Publishing, 2002.

Gravett, Christopher, and Turner, Graham. *English Medieval Knight 1400–1500.* Oxford: Osprey Publishing, 2001.

Griffith, Liddon R. *Mugging: You Can Protect Yourself.* Englewood Cliffs, NJ: Spectrum Books, 1978.

Hancock, H. Irving. *Jiu-jitsu Combat Tricks.* New York: G. Putnam & Sons, 1904.

Hancock, H. Irving, and Higashi, Katsukuma. *The Complete Kano Jiu-jitsu.* New York: Dover Books, 1961 reprint.

Hochheim, W. Hock. *Military Knife Combat.* Ft. Oglethorpe, GA: Lauric Press.

Hochheim, W. Hock. *Knife Fighting Encyclopedia, Vol. 1.* Ft. Oglethorpe, GA: Lauric Press, 2000.

Hockheim, W. Hock. *Unarmed Against the Knife.* Ft. Oglethorpe, GA: Lauric Press, 2001.

Hui, Mizhou. *San Shou Kung Fu of the Chinese Red Army.* Boulder, CO: Paladin Press, 1996.

Hutton, Alfred. *Old Sword Play: Techniques of the Great Masters.* Mineola, NY: Dover, 2001.

Jager, Eric. *The Last Duel.* New York: Broadway Books, 2004.

Janich, Michael D. *Knife Fighting: A Practical Course.* Boulder, CO: Paladin Press, 1993.

Jwing-Ming, Yang. *Analysis of Shaolin Chin Na.* Jamaica Plain, MA: YMAA Publication Center, 1992.

Kano, Jiguro. *Kodokan Judo.* New York: Kodansha International, 1990.

Kirchner, Paul. *Dueling with Sword and Pistol: 400 Years of One-on-One Combat.* Boulder, CO: Paladin Press, 2004.

LaFond, James. *The Logic of Steel.* Boulder, CO: Paladin Press, 2001.

Lo, Man Kam. *Police Kung Fu.* Boston: Tuttle Publishing, 2001.

MacYoung, Marc. *Knives, Knife Fighting, and Related Hassles.* Boulder, CO: Paladin Press, 1990.

Maynard, Russell. *Tanto: Japanese Knives and Knife Fighting.* Burbank, CA: Unique Publications, 1986.

Miller, Stephen G. *Ancient Greek Athletics.* New Haven: Yale University Press, 2004.

Mol, Serge. *Classical Fighting Arts of Japan: A Complete Guide to Koryu Jujutsu.* New York: Kodansha International, 2001.

Myers, Keith. *Medieval Hand-to-Hand Combat.* 2002. (Privately published).

Mysnyk, Mark, et al. *Winning Wrestling Moves.* Champaign, IL: Human Kinetics, 1994.

Nakayama, M., and Draeger, Donn F. *Practical Karate: Against Armed Assailants.* Rutland, VT: Charles E. Tuttle Co., 1964.

Nakayama, M. *Best Karate Vol. 1.* New York: Kodansha International, 1978.

Nakayama, M. *Best Karate Vol. 2.* New York: Kodansha International, 1979.

McLemore, Dwight C. *Bowie and Big-Knife Fighting System.* Boulder, CO: Paladin Press, 2003.

Nicholl, Charles. *The Reckoning: The Murder of Christopher Marlowe.* New York: Harcourt Brace & Co., 1992.

Perkins, John, et al. *Attack Proof.* Champaign, IL: Human Kinetics, 2001.

Peterson, Harold L. *Daggers and Fighting Knives of the Western World: From the Stone Age till 1900.* New York: Walker & Company, 1968.

Rector, Mark. *Highland Swordsmanship.* Union City, CA: Chivalry Bookshelf, 2001.

Roesdahl, Else. *The Vikings.* London: Penguin, 1987.

Sanchez, John. *Slash and Thrust.* Boulder CO: Paladin Press, 1980.

Sato, Hiroaki trans. *The Sword & the Mind.* New York: Barnes & Noble Books, 2004.

Sekunda, Nicholas. *Marathon 490 BC: The First Persian Invasion of Greece.* Oxford, England: Osprey, 2002.

Sharpe, Reginald R., ed. *Calendar of Coroners Rolls of the City of London A.D. 1300–1378.* Suffolk, England: Richard Clay and Sons, 1913.

Shou-Yu, Liang and Ngo, Tai D. *Chinese Fast Wrestling for Fighting: The Art of San Shou Kuai Jiao.* Jamaica Plains, MA: YMAA, 1997.

Shum, Leung. *Eagle Claw Kung Fu.* Boston: Tuttle, 2001.

Siddorn, J. Kim. *Viking Weapons & Warfare.* Charleston, SC: Arcadia Publishing Inc., 2000.

Spindler, Conrad. *The Man in the Ice.* New York: Crown, 1994.

Styers, John. *Cold Steel: Techniques of Close Combat.* Boulder, CO: Paladin Press, reprinted 1974.

Thompson, Christopher. *Lannaireachd: Gaelic Swordsmanship.* 2001.

Thompson, Logan. *Daggers and Bayonets: A History.* Boulder, CO: Paladin Press, 1999.

Tobler, Christian Henry. *Secrets of German Medieval Swordsmanship: Sigmund Ringeck's Commentaries on Master Liechtenauer's Verse.* Chivalry Bookshelf, 2001.

Turnbull, Stephen. *The Knight Triumphant.* London: Cassell & Co., 2001.

U.S. Marine Corps. *Close Combat (MCRP 3-02B).* Washington, DC, 1999.

U.S. Army. *Hand-to-Hand Combat (FM 21-150).* Washington, DC, 1954. Reprinted by Desert Publications, Cornville, AZ.

Underwood, William J. *Self-Defense for Women: Combato.* New York: Avalon Press, 1944.

Underwood, Richard. *Anglo-Saxon Weapons & Warfare.* Charleston, SC: Arcadia Publishing Inc., 2001.

Unknown. *The Rules and Regulations for Sword Exercise for Cavalry 1796.* Ottawa: Museum Restoration Service, 1970.

Vegetius Renatus, Flavius. "The Military Institutions of the Romans," *Roots of Strategy:* Harrisburg, PA, 1985: Stackpole Books, 1985, pp. 67–175.

Vercel, Roger. *Bertrand of Brittany.* New Haven: Yale University Press, 1934.

Wagner, Paul, ed. *Master of Defence: The Works of George Silver.* Boulder, CO: Paladin Press, 2003.

Wagner, Paul, and Hand, Stephen. *Medieval Swordsmanship: The Combat System of Royal Armouries MS I.33.* Union City, CA: Chivalry Bookshelf, 2003.

War Department, *Unarmed Defense for the American Soldier (FM 21-150).* Washington, DC, 1942.

Watson, G.R. *The Roman Soldier.* Ithaca, NY: Cornell University Press, 1969.

Wright, A.D., and Stern, Virginia. *In Search of Christopher Marlowe.* New York: Vanguard Press, 1965.

Xenophon. Betty Radice and Robert Baldick, ed. *The Persian Expedition.* Baltimore: Penguin, 1965.

Yanilov, Eyal. *Krav Maga: How to Defend Yourself Against Armed Assault.* Berkeley, CA: Frog Ltd, 2001.

Yerkow, Charles. *Modern Judo Vol. 1, Basic Techniques.* Harrisburg, PA: Military Service Publishing Co., 1956.

Yerkow, Charles. *Modern Judo Vol. 2, Advanced Techniques.* Harrisburg, PA: Military Service Publishing Co., 1958.

Yerkow, Charles. *Modern Judo: The Complete Ju-Jutsu Library.* Harrisburg, PA: Military Service Publishing Co., 1944.

SECONDARY SOURCES (VIDEOS)

Cunningham, Stephen. *Core Throwing Techniques of the Kodokan Judo Syllabus, Vol. 1.* U.S. Judo Association, 2001.

Cunningham, Stephen. *Core Throwing Techniques of the Kodokan Judo Syllabus, Vol. 2.* U.S. Judo Association, 2001.

Goshin-Jutsu. Tokyo: Kodokan, no date.

Hand to Hand Combat: Marine Corps L.I.N.E.

Training. San Diego, CA: Documentary Recordings, 1999.

Kime-no-kata. Tokyo: Kodokan, no date.

MacYoung, Marc. *Surviving a Street Knife Attack.* Miami, FL: LOTI Production Group, 1995.

Maffei, Joe. *The Reality of Edged Weapons.* Boulder, CO: Paladin Press, 2001.

Medieval Longsword: Basics of German Swordplay. Munich: Flashback Video, 2003.

Quinn, Peyton. *Defending Against the Blade.* Lake George, CO: Curve Productions, 1990.

Surviving Edged Weapons. Northbrook, IL: Calibre Press, 1988.

Tanemura, Shoto. *Kokusai Jujutsu Renmei, Vol. 1–10.* Saitama-Ken, Japan, self-published, 2002.

ABOUT THE AUTHOR

Jason Vail has a B.S. in journalism from the University of Florida and a J.D. from Florida State University. He has worked as a journalist and has written for martial arts and military history publications.

He began his study of martial arts with judo at age 12, and at 18 he began studying karate, which he has trained in for 35 years. He has black belts in taekwon do and Cuong Nhu martial arts, an eclectic system founded by Ngo Dong consisting of elements of Shotokan karate, wing chun, and Vietnamese martial arts.

He began his weapons training with iaido and bojutsu in the late 1970s, shortly afterward turning to Vietnamese staff and spear. He has been studying and interpreting medieval and Renaissance fighting manuals, focusing primarily on the unarmed and armed dagger techniques, since 2001.